PORSCHE

INTRO

Wer 5.700 Kilometer weit durch Chile und Argentinien fährt, erwartet ganz bestimmt keine „CURVES" als prägendes Element dieser Reise. Der Titel unseres Magazins ist für die Patagonien-Durchquerung von Nord nach Süd aber trotzdem nicht fehl am Platz. Herausfordernd geschlungene Passstraßen in den Anden sorgen für reine Fahrfreude-Momente, wie wir sie aus den Alpen oder anderen Gebirgen kennen. Aber natürlich reiht sich diese Ausgabe trotzdem eher unter den bisherigen CURVES-Ausgaben ein, die epische Fernreisen zum Thema haben: Nach den Rocky Mountains, Island oder Thailand folgt nun eine Globetrotter-Pilgerfahrt durch den äußersten Süden des amerikanischen Doppelkontinents. Mit dieser Reise haben wir uns einen lang gehegten Traum erfüllt und hoffen, auch bei Ihnen das Fernweh zu wecken – nach einer Welt, in der sich majestätische Natur mit einer atemberaubenden Vielfalt zeigt und die viele Hunderte von Kilometern weit der Hauptdarsteller ist. Diese Reise erklärt sich am besten mit dem CURVES-Motto: Soulful Driving. Unterwegssein im Flow, in anrührenden Landschaften am Ende der Welt, Abenteuer und Erlebnis in Reinkultur. Die hier vorliegende Ausgabe soll Lust zum eigenen Nachfahren machen, aber auch eine Geschichte erzählen, die für sich allein stehen kann, ein wunderschöner Traum ist. Soulful Driving in Patagonien.
—

Anyone undertaking a 5,700-kilometer drive through Chile and Argentina is almost certainly not expecting "CURVES" to be the defining element of their trip. Nevertheless, the title of our magazine is not entirely inappropriate when traversing Patagonia from north to south. Challengingly winding mountain pass roads through the Andes guarantee moments of pure driving pleasure, a familiar feeling from the Alps or other mountain terrain. But of course this issue fits perfectly with the previous issues of CURVES that have focused on epic long-distance journeys: after the Rocky Mountains, Iceland or Thailand we now find ourselves on a globetrotting pilgrimage through the extreme south of the Americas. This journey marked the fulfillment of a long-cherished dream and we hope that our account will awaken an ambition to travel among our readers, a yearning for a world in which majestic nature reveals itself in breath-taking variety and where the hundreds of kilometers play the role of the main protagonist. This trip is best explained with the CURVES motto: soulful driving. On the move and in the flow in heart-stopping landscapes at the ends of the earth, adventure and experience at its purest. This issue is intended to whet your appetite for your own personal journey, but also tells a story that stands in its own right, a beautiful dream. Soulful driving in Patagonia.

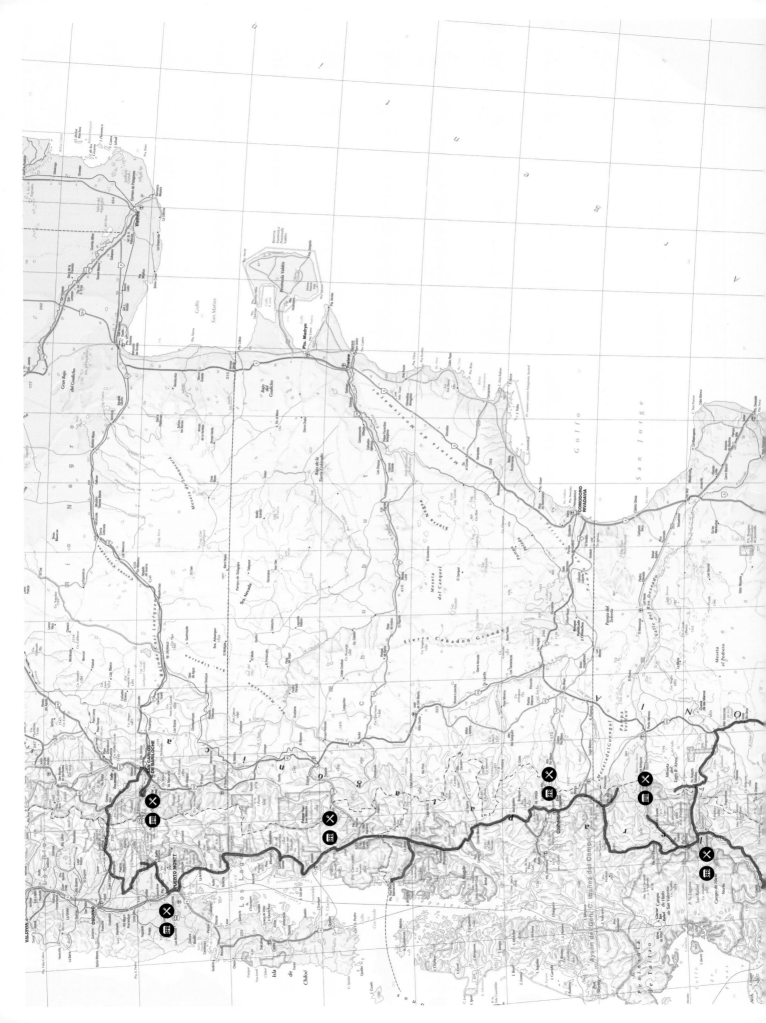

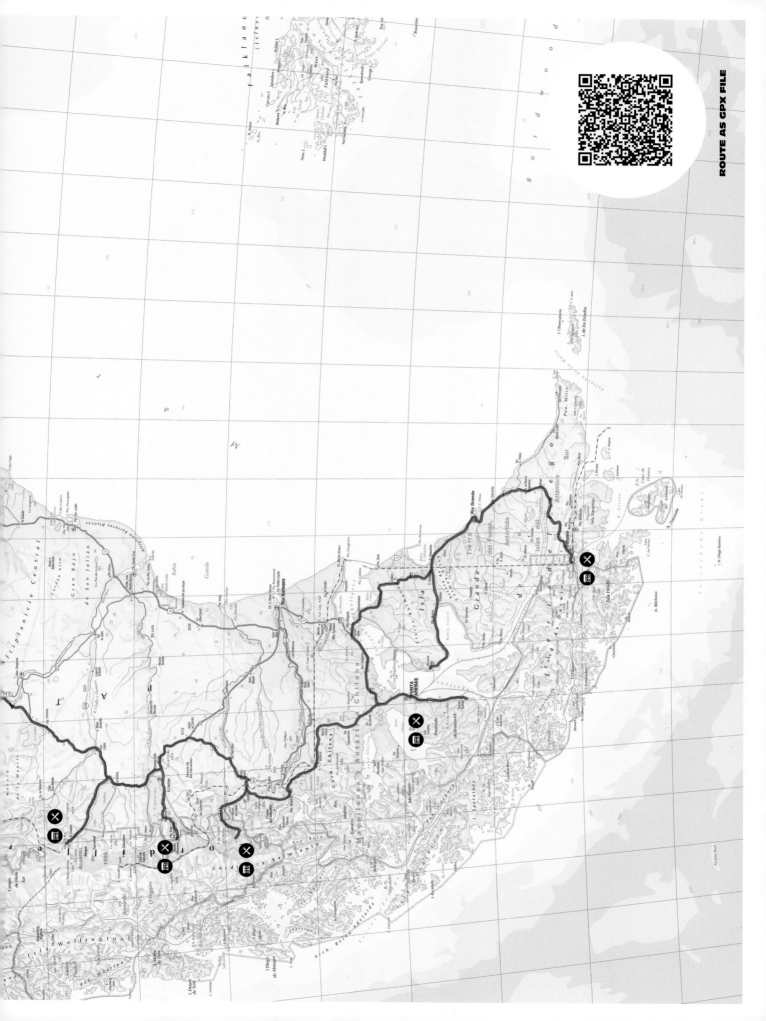

ROUTE AS GPX FILE

PASO RÍO DON GUILLERMO

ETAPPE
STAGE

ETAPPE
STAGE

Mit dem 320-Kilometer-Ausflug über die Anden, hinüber nach Bariloche, setzen wir einen ganz bewussten Auftakt an den Beginn unserer Reise durch Patagonien. Anstatt der „Carretera Austral" nach Süden zu folgen, ziehen wir nach Osten, gegen den Strich der Berge. Auf dem Weg in die „Schweiz Argentiniens" überqueren wir den Anden-Hauptkamm in ganzer Breite und gelangen am östlichen Fuß des Gebirges bis an die weiten Ebenen der argentinischen Pampa. Nicht nur die spannende Fahrt in den Kurven der Nationalparks macht diesen Auftakt-Abstecher für uns zur Pflicht, auch der Besuch Bariloches ist einen Umweg wert. Die Stadt steht beinahe sinnbildlich für die Geschichte Patagoniens: Mit den deutlich wahrnehmbaren Einflüssen deutscher Einwanderer, ihrer Geschichte als ehemaligem Handelsposten im Land der Ureinwohner und der heutigen Leuchtturm-Rolle im Outdoor-Tourismus spiegelt die Departamento-Hauptstadt der Provinz Rio Negro das Werden vieler Städte Patagoniens wider. Zurück am Ausgangspunkt, in Puerto Montt, geht die eigentliche Fahrt nach Süden los – mit einer Etappe entlang der Fjorde am Pazifik. Fährschiffe spielen hier immer wieder eine prägende Rolle, das Déjà-vu für Norwegen-Fans ist unausweichlich.

Rund 750 Kilometer liegen zwischen Chaitén am Golf von Corcovado und den Gletschergebieten rund um Cochrane, im Süden der Region de Aisén. Wer diese Strecke auf der Carretera Austral befahren möchte, sollte sich auf mehrere Tagesetappen und eine abwechslungsreiche Gangart einstellen. Weite Teile der Strecke sind immer wieder nicht asphaltiert, führen durch menschenleere Gebiete und über anspruchsvolles Terrain. Im Norden wird die Straße von Vulkanen eskortiert, strebt dann vorbei am Corcovado-Nationalpark durch die Región de los Lagosbis zum Puyuhuapi-Fjord, der vom Pazifik her weit ins Landesinnere einschneidet. Hier ändert sich die Richtung der Fernstraße, sie überquert in mehreren Zügen den Anden-Hauptkamm, bis sie bei Coyhaique am östlichen Fuß des Gebirgszugs angelangt ist. Durch die Región de Aysén geht es nun weiter nach Süden, rund um den riesigen Lago General Carrera, der in seinem östlichen, argentinischen Teil „Lago Buenos Aires" genannt wird, dann wieder etwas weiter ins Hochgebirge zurück. In Cochrane haben wir das Ziel unserer Etappe erreicht – und auch beinahe das Ende der Carretera Austral.

The 320-kilometer journey across the Andes to Bariloche is a very deliberate curtain-raiser to our journey through Patagonia. Instead of following the "Carretera Austral" south, we head east, in the opposite direction to the mountains. On the way to the "Switzerland of Argentina" we cross the entire width of the main Andes ridge, eventually reaching the eastern foot of the mountains and the wide plains of the Argentine pampas. This initial detour is made worthwhile for us not just by the exciting curves as we drive through the national park, but also by the chance to visit Bariloche. The city is almost symbolic of the history of Patagonia: With the clearly perceptible influences of German immigrants, its history as a former trading post among the indigenous populations and its modern flagship role in outdoor tourism, the capital of the Rio Negro province reflects the development of many of Patagonia's cities and towns. Back at our starting point in Puerto Montt, the actual journey south begins with a stage that closely follows the Pacific fjords. Ferries play a formative role, so that a feeling of déjà vu is inevitable for Norway fans.

A distance of around 750 kilometers lies between Chaitén on the Gulf of Corcovado and the glacier fields around Cochrane, in the south of the Aisén region. If you intend to drive this route on the Carretera Austral, you should be prepared for a number of daily stages and a varied pace. Large parts of the route are unpaved and lead through desert areas and across challenging terrain. In the north, the road runs past several volcanoes, then traverses the Corcovado National Park and the Región de los Lagos to reach the Puyuhuapi Fjord, which cuts far inland from the Pacific. The direction of the highway changes here, crossing the main Andes ridge in several stretches until it arrives at Coyhaique at the eastern foot of the mountain range. Passing through the Región de Aysén we continue south, around the huge Lago General Carrera, the eastern, Argentinian part of which is called "Lago Buenos Aires", then head back a little further into the high mountains. In Cochrane we reach the end of this particular stage – and almost the end of the Carretera Austral.

3 ETAPPE STAGE

Lago Argentino, Lago Viedma und Lago O'Higgins/Lago San Martin: Diese drei gewaltigen Gletscherseen sind die Speicher des Schmelzwassers einer riesigen Eiskappe über den Anden. Und sie machen sich direkt auf unserer Route von Nord nach Süd breit, lassen kein Durchkommen. Unsere Route geht deshalb pragmatisch vor: Nach einem Besuch der Fjordlandschaft rund um die Bajo Pisagua fahren wir auf der Carretera Austral in Richtung Norden, dann Osten, überqueren die Grenze nach Argentinien und rollen dann in der weiten Pampa nach Süden. Auf dieser Umgehungsroute ist enormes Sitzfleisch notwendig, die nahezu endlos wirkenden Kilometer auf den Straßen durch die südamerikanische Hochlandsteppe können zermürbend sein. Allerdings ist von dieser Seite des Gebirges her ein guter Zugang zu den atemberaubenden Schönheiten Patagoniens möglich: den Bergen Fitz Roy und Cerro Torre westlich von El Chaitén, sowie den Gletschern in den Seitenarmen des Lago Argentino. Und während sich diese spektakulären Sehenswürdigkeiten in unseren Reise-Erinnerungen fest einnisten, schaffen das am Ende auch die Kilometer durch die Pampa: als magisches Gefühl, als Ahnung von ungeheurer Weite. Das Ziel unserer Etappe liegt in Torres del Paine – einem unscheinbaren Ort zwischen Pampa und Bergen, aber wieder am Tor zu einem Wunder Patagoniens.

Lago Argentino, Lago Viedma and Lago O'Higgins/Lago San Martin: these three mighty glacial lakes are the reservoirs of meltwater from a huge ice cap that covers the Andes. And they spread out directly on our route from north to south, blocking our path. Our route therefore involves a pragmatic approach: after a visit to the fjord landscape around Bajo Pisagua, we head north on the Carretera Austral, then east, cross the border into Argentina and then roll south through the wide pampas. Enormous patience is required on this bypass route, as the seemingly endless distances on the roads through the South American highland steppes can be grueling. However, this side of the mountain range offers plenty of access to the breathtaking beauties of Patagonia: the Fitz Roy and Cerro Torre mountains west of El Chaitén, as well as the glaciers in the side arms of Lago Argentino. While these spectacular sights are firmly embedded in our travel memories, the distance traveled through the pampas also plays its part in the end: a magical feeling, an impression of immense vastness. The final destination of this stage is in Torres del Paine – an unremarkable spot between the pampas and the mountain, but yet another gateway to the wonders of Patagonia.

4 ETAPPE STAGE

Die wilde und unvergleichliche Schönheit des Nationalparks Torres del Paine macht ihn zu einer der bekanntesten und meistbesuchten Gegenden Patagoniens. Wer den Park also nicht mit vielen anderen Besuchern teilen möchte, sollte trotz des dann eher sicheren Wetters mit Temperaturen bis 20 Grad Celsius und tendenziell weniger Niederschlag nicht im Sommer anreisen. Vorsicht bei der Planung: Wegen der Lage Patagoniens auf der Südhalbkugel liegen die Sommermonate im Dezember und Februar … Für einen Besuch im Winter – also Juni bis August – sollte man sich auf kaltes und verregnetes Wetter einstellen, darüber hinaus sind die Tage ausgesprochen kurz. Der Frühling hat seinen Reiz, unser Geheimtipp wäre aber ein Besuch im Herbst, von März bis Mai. Jetzt verfärbt sich die Vegetation reizvoll, das Wetter kann sonnige Momente haben und Unterkünfte findet man auch noch etwas spontaner, ohne lange Vorbuchzeit. Auf unserem weiteren Weg nach Süden zeigt sich Patagonien aber ebenfalls von einer spannenden Seite. Selbst ohne die spektakulären Naturattraktionen der Parks in den Anden strahlt das weite Land der Pampa und Tundra eine eigentümliche und anziehende Ruhe und Tiefe aus, es ist dünn besiedelt und oft menschenleer. Hier, im Süden des Südens, endet unsere Reise in der südlichsten Stadt des Kontinents: Ushuaia.

The wild and incomparable beauty of Torres del Paine National Park makes it one of the most famous and most visited areas of Patagonia. Consequently, if you don't want to share the park with lots of other visitors, you shouldn't travel there in summer, despite the more predictable weather, with temperatures up to 20 degrees Celsius and less rainfall. Be careful when laying your plans: because of Patagonia's location in the southern hemisphere, the summer months are from December to February… For a visit in winter – i.e. June to August – you should be prepared for cold and rainy weather, as well as extremely short days. Spring has its charms, but our insider tip would be to visit in the fall, from March to May. That's when the vegetation changes color in an attractive way, the weather can have sunny moments and accommodation can be found a little more easily, without having to book long in advance. As we continue south, Patagonia also shows an exciting side. Even without the spectacular natural attractions of the parks in the Andes, the vast area of pampas and tundra exudes a peculiar and alluring calm and depth. Here, in the very southernmost point, our journey ends in the most southerly city on the continent, Ushuaia.

PERITO-MORENO-GLETSCHER

EDITORIAL

Patagonien, die Landschaft im Süden von Argentinien und Chile, ist eine riesige Welt aus Sonne und Licht, aus Bergen und Steppen, aus Eis und Wasser. Aus der Ferne ein Mythos, gläsern, unwirklich und ätherisch, aus der Nähe aber super-real. Hyper-präsent. Larger than life.

Lavagraue Vulkane dulden Kappen aus Schnee und Eis, ragen aus geröllübersäten Landschaften, rumoren mit Magma-gefüllten Bäuchen und rauchen aus kilometertiefen Schloten. Türkis leuchtende Eisberge, die Kinder zerfurchter Gletscher, lösen sich knirschend und knackend, gleiten gischtend ins Wasser magischer Fjorde, über denen schneebedeckte Gebirge in azurblauen Himmel ragen. Einsame Flüsse winden sich in den weiten Trögen von unaufhörlich zwischen Hügelketten voranstrebenden Tälern, murmeln mit Geröll, schneiden Stein, ernähren das Land.

Ganze Landschaften sind überzogen vom dichten Pelz gelben, trockenen Grases, das in einem unaufhörlichen Wind von Westen her tanzt und flirrt und schillert und leuchtet, ein tausendjähriges Schaudern der Erde aus Gras. Federweiße Wolken sammeln sich in den unsichtbaren Strömen der Atmosphäre, formen Raumschiffe und Drachen oder türmen sich zu Giganten, die bis in die Stratosphäre reichen, während ihre dampfenden Sockel triefende Gebirge benetzen und über weite Ebenen rasen. Farmhäuser ducken sich in den Wind, nisten sich im Schutz von Hügelkämmen ein und verschanzen sich hinter einem Labyrinth aus Viehweiden mit mürben Zäunen. Die riesigen Lachen absurd blauer Seen schwappen in einem Meer aus Steppe, während der Wind ihren Oberflächen gischtende Krönchen aus weißem Schaum aufsetzt. Aus fernem Dunst wogen Fjorde heran, schneiden breit und tief ins Land am Pazifik – ein dreister Landraub, misstrauisch beobachtet von bewaldeten Hängen –, während sich in Jahrzehnten verdrehte Baumriesen an den Kiesufern tief übers Wasser beugen, als wollten sie einen Blick in den Spiegel des Wassers werfen. Schwärme von Kondoren surfen in flackernden Aufwinden, schwarze Scheren-

Patagonia, the region in the south of Argentina and Chile, is an immense domain of sunshine and light, mountains and steppes, ice and water. Considered from a distance, it has a mythical quality, fragile, unreal and ethereal. Seen at close quarters, however, it is super-real, hyper-present and larger than life.

Volcanoes encrusted with gray lava patiently accept a dressing of snow and ice as they rise out of jumbled landscapes of rubble, their magma-filled bellies rumbling loudly, breathing smoke from their unfathomable abysses. Glaciers, mountains of luminous turquoise ice, loosen from their moorings with a crunching, cracking sound like the stuff of children's nightmares, sliding gracefully into the waters of magical fjords, surrounded by snow-capped mountain peaks and azure-blue skies. Lonely rivers wind their way insistently through the broad valleys formed between the mountain ranges, murmuring to the gentle clatter of rolling pebbles, cutting a path through the rocky surroundings to nourish the land.

Entire landscapes are wrapped in a thick coat of dry yellow grasses that wave endlessly in the western wind in a dance that has continued uninterrupted for millennia. Feather-white clouds gather in the invisible atmosphere, forming into spaceships and dragons or climbing as gigantic towers that stretch to the stratosphere, while their lower parts drench the mountains with rain as they rush onward across the wide plains. Farmhouses crouch low against the wind, sheltering in the lee of mountain ridges, and cowering behind a labyrinth of rickety-fenced cattle pastures. The vast, absurdly blue lakes provide some variation in a sea of steppe, while the wind whips the surface of the water into crowns of white foam. Billowing fjords emerge from a distant haze, cutting wide and deep into the Pacific coastline in a brazen land grab. All the while, twisting giant ancient trees watch suspiciously from the hillsides or bend low over the water on the shingle shore, as

schnitte vor Blau. Duftende Nadelwälder graben Wurzeln tief in dumpf tönende Erde, ein paar Kilometer weiter senden die Farben von Blättern Morsezeichen als atemberaubend buntes Kaleidoskop von Schönheit. Das unermesslich intensive Land Patagoniens lässt sich aber nicht nur auf diese wilde und weite Natur einhegen. Die romantisierende Illusion vollkommener Menschenleere und friedlicher Unberührtheit entspricht eher einem modernen Wunschdenken als der Realität. Patagonien gehört zur Welt der Menschen, ganz definitiv. Bereits 8.000 bis 10.000 Jahre vor unserer Zeitrechnung landeten Jägergruppen aus dem Norden in Feuerland, der südlichsten Gegend dieses entfernten Teils der Welt, und ließen sich trotz des harten Klimas nieder. Gehörten für Jahrhunderte und Jahrtausende zu den Ökosystem-Gezeiten einer dramatischen und harten Umwelt, bis sich im 19. Jahrhundert die Europäer das Ende der Welt vornahmen: Die Stämme der Haush und Selk'nam im Osten des Landes und die der Kawesqar oder Yámana im pazifischen Osten hatten dem Ansturm der Profiteure und Missionare, der Schafzüchter und Glücksritter, ihren eingeschleppten Seuchen und Kopfgeldprämien nichts entgegenzusetzen. Nach Jahrtausenden von nomadischer Besiedlung des Landes wurden die Ureinwohner innerhalb eines knappen Jahrhunderts nahezu vollkommen ausgerottet. Heute leben nur noch wenige Angehörige der uralten Stämme. Oder keine mehr.

Dabei wurden Patagonien und seine südlichste Provinz Feuerland sogar nach ihren Ureinwohnern benannt: Der portugiesisch-spanische Entdecker Ferdinand Magellan überwinterte in der Meeresstraße zwischen dem kontinentalen Festland und den Feuerland-Inseln im Jahr 1520, er soll dabei von der Größe einiger Ureinwohner so verblüfft gewesen sein, dass er ihr Land nach dem sagenhaften Riesen Pathagón benannte: Patagonien. Historische Logbücher geben an, die europäischen Seefahrer hätten südlich der heutigen Magellan-Straße keine Menschen gesichtet, allerdings seien bei Nacht unzählige Lagerfeuer auf dieser Isla Grande de Tierra del Fuego zu sehen gewesen – dem Feuerland eben.

Dass damit selbst die Namen des Landes an ihre ehemaligen Bewohner erinnern, aus der naiven, grausamen und anmaßenden Perspektive der

if waiting to catch a glimpse of themselves in the mirrored surface. Flocks of condors hang in the wavering thermal currents, black silhouettes against the blue sky. Fragrant evergreen forests bury their roots deep into muted earth, a couple of kilometers further on, the colors of the leaves provide a breath-taking kaleidoscope of beauty like Technicolor Morse code.

The immeasurable intensity of Patagonia is not confined to its wild and diverse natural bounty. The romantic illusion of a complete remote, peaceful and unspoiled state is more a product of modern wishful thinking than reality. Patagonia is undeniably part of the real world. As early as 8,000 to 10,000 years BC, groups of hunter-gatherers from the north landed in Tierra del Fuego, the southernmost region of this remote part of the world, and settled there despite the harsh climate. They formed part of the ecosystem of this harsh and dramatic environment for centuries and millennia, until the 19th century, when Europeans infiltrated this end of the world: the Haush and Selk'nam tribes in the east of the country and the Kawesqar or Yámana on the Pacific east coast had nothing to ward off the onslaught of profiteers and missionaries, sheep farmers and soldiers of fortune with their imported diseases and bounty rewards. After thousands of years of nomadic settlement of the country, the indigenous people were almost completely exterminated within a century. Only a few members of the ancient tribes survive today. If any.

Patagonia and its southernmost province of Tierra del Fuego were actually named after their native peoples: Portuguese-Spanish explorer Ferdinand Magellan over-wintered in the straits between the continental mainland and the islands of Tierra del Fuego in 1520, and is said to have been so amazed by the tall stature of some of the native people that he named their country after the legendary giant Pathagón: Patagonia. Historical logbooks state that European seafarers did not encounter any people south of today's Strait of Magellan, but countless campfires could be seen at night here on Isla Grande de Tierra del Fuego – the land of fire. The fact that even the names of the country are reminders of their former inhabitants, from the naive,

europäischen Eroberer, gehört zur Geschichte Patagoniens. Vielleicht ist es vor diesem Hintergrund ja die eigentlich sehr deutliche Botschaft der unfassbar weiten und wilden Natur Patagoniens, die uns den entscheidenden Hinweis ins Logbuch schreibt: Nur mit viel Demut hat die Menschheit eine Zukunft.

Der Übergang in diese Welt ist ein kurzer Prozess: Du machst einfach alle Leinen los, setzt die Segel und sofort treibt dich ein Wind aus unbändiger Reiselust unaufhaltsam vor sich her. Zuerst akzeptierst du die vielen Kilometer in stetigem Rhythmus als maßgebenden Aggregatzustand, wartest auf die Höhepunkte in einem ruhig dahinfließenden Reise-Marathon – und dann stellst du plötzlich fest, dass diese Autopilot-Erwartung ganz falsch ist. Denn das Unterwegssein in Patagonien kennt keine Längen. Keine Wiederholungen. Nur eine atemberaubende Vielfalt an Eindrücken von solcher Dichte und Intensität, dass einem immer wieder die Werkzeuge fehlen, um alles zu verarbeiten. Die Worte. Die Vergleiche. Die Maßstäbe. Gewöhnen tut man sich an diesen Überfluss bemerkenswerter Erfahrungen eigentlich nie, ab einem gewissen Punkt wandelt sich das wiederkehrende Staunen lediglich in pures Glück. Patagonien macht ausgeglichen und still, schrumpft den Reisenden gesund. Das Woher und Wohin, der Blick in den Rückspiegel und der Horizont voraus werden zu irrelevanten Größen. Immer mehr zählt nur das Jetzt. Der Moment.

Gut, dass wir in diesem Tagtraum immer wieder bekannte Größen entdecken: die Menschen, durch deren Land, durch deren Städte und Dörfer wir unterwegs sind. Ihre gelassene und freundliche Art. Ihre unaufdringliche Neugier auf die Reisenden. Das, was man Gastfreundschaft nennt und in Patagonien von unaufgeregter Offenheit geprägt ist. Mapuche, Spanisch, Deutsch – hier treffen sich Alte und Neue Welt, krasse Gegensätze und überraschende Parallelen, Denkweisen und Perspektiven, bilden eine ganz eigene kulturelle Identität. Wer eine Abkürzung ins Erleben dieser Identität sucht, sollte die naheliegendste Route einschlagen: Essen. Star der Küche Patagoniens ist das Asado, eine urwüchsige Barbecue-Variante. Allerdings wird hier nicht wie in den nördlicheren Gegenden Argentiniens Rindfleisch gegrillt, sondern vor allem Lamm. Auf der patagonischen Steppe gezüchtet, wird es mit Marinaden auf Basis von Knoblauch, Petersilie, gemahlenem Chili, Rosmarin und Minze kombiniert, schafft es aber nicht nur auf die Asado-Grills, sondern auch in den Ofen oder

cruel and presumptuous perspective of the European conquerors, is part of the history of Patagonia. Against this background, perhaps it is the actually very clear message of the incredibly vast and wild nature of Patagonia that provides the decisive clue in our logbook: mankind needs a great deal of humility if we are to have a future.

The transition to this world does not take long: simply let go all ropes, hoist your sails and you'll immediately find yourself carried forward by an irrepressible desire to travel. At first you accept the steady rhythm of the many kilometers covered in a general dazed state, as you await the highlights on a smooth marathon journey. Then you suddenly realize that this passively expectant autopilot mode is completely wrong. After all, distance means nothing when you take to the road in Patagonia. There are no repetitions, just a breathtaking variety of impressions of such complexity and intensity that you often lack the means to process everything, whether in words, comparisons or standards. You never really get used to this abundance of remarkable experiences, so that after a certain point the recurring amazement simply turns to pure happiness. Patagonia brings balance and calm, confining the traveler's world in the best possible way. It no longer matters where you've come from or where you're going to. The sights in the rear-view mirror and the horizon up ahead become irrelevant factors. More and more you'll find that all that counts is the now, the current moment.

It's a good thing that we keep discovering familiar elements in this daydream: the people through whose country, towns and villages we are traveling. We're struck by their relaxed and friendly manner and their unobtrusive curiosity about the travelers they meet. Hospitality in Patagonia is characterized by a calm openness. Mapuche, Spanish, German – this is where the old and new worlds collide in stark contrasts and surprising parallels, ways of thinking and perspectives, forming a totally unique cultural identity. Anyone looking for a shortcut to experiencing this identity should take the most obvious route: food. The star of Patagonian cuisine is asado, a native variant of barbecue. However, beef is not the main grilled meat here as in the northern regions of Argentina, but mostly lamb. Bred on the Patagonian steppe, lamb is combined with marinades based on garlic, parsley, ground chili, rosemary and mint. As well as being a favorite ingredient in asado grills, it is also used in roasts or stews.

Zuerst akzeptierst du die vielen Kilometer in stetigem Rhythmus als maßgebenden Aggregatzustand, wartest auf die Höhepunkte in einem ruhig dahinfließenden Reise-Marathon – und dann stellst du plötzlich fest, dass diese Autopilot-Erwartung ganz falsch ist. Denn das Unterwegssein in Patagonien kennt keine Längen. Keine Wiederholungen. Nur eine atemberaubende Vielfalt an Eindrücken von solcher Dichte und Intensität, dass einem immer wieder die Werkzeuge fehlen, um alles zu verarbeiten. Die Worte. Die Vergleiche. Die Maßstäbe.

At first you accept the steady rhythm of the many kilometers covered in a general dazed state, as you await the highlights on a smooth marathon journey. Then you suddenly realize that this passively expectant autopilot mode is completely wrong. After all, distance means nothing when you take to the road in Patagonia. There are no repetitions, just a breathtaking variety of impressions of such complexity and intensity that you often lack the means to process everything, whether in words, comparisons or standards.

in Eintöpfe. Anders als man angesichts der Lage Patagoniens am Pazifik vermuten könnte, spielen Fisch und Meeresfrüchte eher eine Nebenrolle, die Qualität des großen Angebots an maritimen Köstlichkeiten ist aber bemerkenswert. In Hafenrestaurants landet frisch gefangener Fisch an, vor allem aber die Antarktische Königskrabbe sollte man unbedingt probieren. Aus den Kochtöpfen der Ureinwohner haben es Bohnen, Kartoffeln und Mais ins Angebot der patagonischen Küche geschafft, die vielen deutschen Einwanderer steuern unter anderem Brot, Würste und Kuchen bei. Ausgezeichnetes Bier wird hier ebenfalls gebraut. Dass durch Patagonien aber sogar eine „Weinstraße" führt, dürfte nicht weithin bekannt sein.

Ein internationaler Star Südamerikas mit durchschlagender Karriere ist die Schokolade – und natürlich wird sie auch in Patagonien verehrt. Eine weitere Spezialität ist zwar weltweit bekannt und bei Insidern geschätzt, gehört aber nach wie vor eher zur kulinarischen Folklore Südamerikas: der Mate-Tee. Die getrockneten und geschnittenen Blätter des Mate-Baums werden bei seiner Zubereitung in einer kleinen Kalebasse mit heißem Wasser übergossen, der Aufguss dann durch ein Bombilla-Trinkröhrchen mit kleinem Sieb geschlürft. Bitter, krautig, rauchig. Auch in Patagonien ist der Mate-Tee ein regelmäßiges Alltags-Ritual. Zum wundervollen Land am Ende der Welt passt er mit seiner Urwüchsigkeit ausgezeichnet.

Contrary to what you might expect given Patagonia's Pacific coastline, fish and seafood play a secondary role, however the quality of the wide range of maritime delicacies is remarkable. Freshly caught fish can be enjoyed in harbor restaurants, but you should definitely try the Antarctic king crab. Beans, potatoes and corn have made it into Patagonian cuisine from native cooking traditions, while the many German immigrants contributed bread, sausages and cake, among other things. Excellent beer is also brewed here. The fact that there is even a "wine route" through Patagonia is something that is not widely known.

Chocolate is an internationally recognized star in the firmament of South American cuisine and is naturally also revered in Patagonia. Another specialty drawn from the culinary folklore of South America that is familiar throughout the world and much appreciated by aficionados is mate tea. The dried and shredded leaves of the mate tree are steeped in hot water in a small calabash during preparation, and the infusion is then imbibed through a small sieve with a bombilla drinking straw. With its bitter, smoky, herbal flavor, mate tea is also a regular fixture of everyday life in Patagonia. The earthy nature of mate is the perfect fit for this wonderful country at the end of the world.

NATIONALPARK LAGUNA
SAN RAFAEL

FITZ ROY

TORRES DEL PAINE

CARRETERA AUSTRAL
RIO RAYAS

TORRES DEL PAINE

VOLCÁN OSORNO

PERITO-MORENO-GLETSCHER

PUERTO MONTT CHAITÉN

996 KM • 3 TAGE // 619 MILES • 3 DAYS

Wasserwelt. Graue Wolken-Federkissen schwappen in endloser Zeitlupe über den Himmel. Pazifische Wassermassen treffen auf eiskalte Anden, auf trockenes Landesinneres hinter dem Gebirge. Verdunsten und Kondensieren in Endlosschleife, angetrieben von tausende Kilometer weit reichenden Winden. Wetter-Perpetuummobile, beinahe.

—

We find ourselves in a watery world. Gray clouds like weightless feather pillows cross the sky in an endless loop. Pacific water masses collide with the ice-cold Andes and the dry interior terrain beyond the mountains in a continuous process of evaporation and condensation, driven by winds whistling through the air for thousands of kilometers. It's almost as if the weather has cracked the secret of perpetual motion.

HOTELS

HOTEL CUMBRES PUERTO VARAS
AV. IMPERIAL 0561,
PUERTO VARAS, LOS LAGOS
WWW.CUMBRESPUERTOVARAS.COM

....

RESTAURANT

EL BODEGÓN,
LA VINOTECA PUERTO VARAS
DIEGO PORTALES 204,
5550458 PUERTO VARAS, LOS LAGOS,
WWW.LAVINOTECA.CL/TIENDAS

....

Durch eine schmale Lücke in der Wolken-decke dringen Sonnenstrahlen in den Trog des Golf von Ancud – an der Westküste Chiles verschanzt sich diese riesige Bucht hinter der Chiloé-Insel vor dem offenen Pazifik. In ihrem Norden haben sich Seen ins Gebirge eingelagert, der riesige Lago Llanquihue liegt bereits wenige Kilometer entfernt im Hinterland.

Puerto Montt, die Stadt am Meer hinter den Bergen, ist Startpunkt unserer Reise. Aber auch das Ende einer anderen: Hier endet die „Panamericana", Amerikas großes Schnellstraßen-Netz, das sich vom hohen Norden in Alaska bis hier unten erstreckt. Über 25.000 Kilometer Freiheit, schier endlose Bewegung. Die Anden Patagoniens und die Fjorde des Pazifiks verstellen der routiniert heranbrausenden Panamericana aber den Weg, für die letzte Etappe hinunter an die Südspitze Feuerlands muss sich der Reisende der Ruta 7 „Carretera Austral" anvertrauen. Sie ist eine wilde Gefährtin. Ein ungestümes Wesen mit Hang zum Drama, geschottert, geflickt, zerfurcht, geschunden von Wind und Wetter. Bevor wir uns aber mit ihr auf den weiten Weg nach Süden machen, haben wir noch einen Umweg zum Auftakt vor: durchs Land der Seen, Kurs Nordost, dann über die Grenze nach Argentinien hinüber. Nach Bariloche. In die kleine Schweiz Südamerikas, wie die Gegend da oben gern genannt wird. „Schweiz" – das kennen wir. Das sagt uns etwas. CURVES hat sich in den Alpen erfunden, und vielleicht ist dieser Auftakt deshalb also auch so etwas wie schüchternes Eingrooven auf bekanntem Terrain. Bevor es wirklich ins Unbekannte geht.

Große Reisemaschinen warten auf uns, mit Platz für Abenteuer-großes Gepäck und mit groben Reifen. Schließlich werden uns die Straßen und Pisten nicht schonen, da sollte man sich auf bissfestes Material verlassen können. Ein ungewohntes Gefühl ist das, schließlich ziehen wir normalerweise mit leichtem, agilem Gerät durchs Land, aber wir haben uns angewöhnt, auf die Ratschläge der Einheimischen zu hören. Und die wissen, dass die Schotterstraßen im Süden Karosserien sandstrahlen, Fahrwerke mit Schlaglöchern schinden, tückisch Reifen fressen. Aber das liegt jetzt alles noch

Rays of sunlight force their way through a narrow gap in the blanket of cloud to reach the Gulf of Ancud. This immense bay on Chile's west coast takes refuge behind Chiloé Island from the wild, open Pacific. To the north, lakes have formed in the mountains – gigantic Lago Llanquihue is just a few kilometers away in the hinterlands.

Puerto Montt, the coastal town on the other side of the mountains is the place where our journey begins. It is also the end of another journey: this is the end of the line for the "Panamericana", America's vast network of highways that stretches from the north in Alaska to these southern climes. More than 25,000 kilometers of freedom and sheer endless movement. However, the Patagonian Andes and the fjords of the Pacific put a stop to the gallop of the normally fast-paced Panamericana and the final stretch of the journey to the south tip of Tierra del Fuego switches to Route 7 known as "Carretera Austral". This road is a wild and impetuous travelling companion with a penchant for drama, part gravel track, patched and furrowed, battered by wind and rain. But before we set out on the long journey south, we have one more detour in mind: this will take us through the land of lakes, heading north-east, then across the border to Bariloche in Argentina. We are aware that this area is known as South America's little Switzerland, which already tells us a lot. CURVES was conceived in the Alps, and perhaps that's why this curtain-raiser represents something like the first tentative steps in familiar terrain, before we really plunge into the unknown.

The vehicles that await us are genuine travel behemoths with plenty of space for adventure-sized luggage and a set of sturdy tires. After all, the roads and tracks we follow won't offer us much protection, so we need to rely on quality materials. This is a strange feeling, as we normally use light and agile vehicles on our travels; however we have learned to heed the advice of the locals. They know only too well that the gravel roads to the south will sandblast a car's bodywork, punch holes in its chassis and eat away hungrily at its tires. But that's all ahead of us as we cruise along

in der Zukunft, wir fliegen auf dem regelmäßigen Doppelspurband der Panamericana in Richtung Norden. Rechts ragt der Calbuco aus der grünen Ebene empor, ein Vulkan mit zerklüfteter Spitze, die er sich in schöner Regelmäßigkeit bei Ausbrüchen bis in die Stratosphäre sprengt. Seine uralter Lavasockel verläuft bis ans Ufer des Llanquihue-Sees, der hier oben himmelblau-unschuldig so tut, als sei er das Meer selbst: riesengroß, mit Ufern, die von der jeweils gegenüberliegenden Seite beinahe nicht gesehen werden. Nur der zweite Vulkan dieser imposanten Nachbarschaft dient als Wahrzeichen und Navigationspunkt: der Osorno. Dessen präzise geformter Kegel mit der schneebedeckten Spitze erinnert verblüffend an den japanischen Mount Fuji, immer wieder schauen wir auf der Fahrt ums Nordufer des Lago Llanquihue zu ihm hinüber und staunen über diesen Vulkan-Doppelgänger. Das Land ist weit, die Felder unterteilt von Hecken, Zäunen und Baumrandstreifen. Fette Wiesen und üppige Weiden gehören zu einer Vielzahl von Gehöften, Flussläufe winden sich verträumt durch saftige Auen, um dann in den Tiefen des weiten Lago Llanquihue zu verschwinden.

Am Nordufer des Sees streben wir weiter, wechseln auf kleine Landstraßen, die nach Osten ziehen, und streifen kurz die Westspitze des Lago Rupanco. Wenige Kilometer weiter nördlich sind wir bereits am Puyehue-See angelangt, dessen Ostende tief in einem Gebirgstal liegt – dorthin wollen wir. Üppig grüne Wiesen drängen sich ins weite Tal, die Berghänge links und rechts scheinen zuerst noch in weiter Ferne, dann rücken sie zusammen. Ganz beiläufig umzingeln dicht bewaldete Hügelketten die Straße, zwingen sie zu Ausweichbewegungen, schließlich langsam in die Höhe. Auch die weiten Auen unten im Tal bleiben zurück, beinahe unmerklich hat sich dichte Baumvegetation bis an den Straßenrand geschoben und jetzt geht es los: Die bisher noch entspannt drauflos schlendernde Straße nimmt Fahrt auf. Bröckelnder und geflickter Asphalt schiebt gewaltig voran, kurvt in dichtem Subtropen-Regenwald immer höher hinauf. Die Atmosphäre dieses Walds ist eigentümlich, ständig flackern Erinnerungen an andere Reisen in uns auf, die innere Kompassnadel dreht sich verwirrt:

the regular two-lane highway of the Panamericana, heading north. To the right, the craggy-tipped cauldron of the Calbuco rises from the greenery. This volcano is known to erupt at regular intervals, throwing plumes of ash and smoke into the stratosphere. Its ancient lava base spreads as far as the shores of Lago Llanquihue, whose waters are such a vibrant, innocent sky blue that you would almost think you were looking at the sea itself: this is a truly enormous body of water, its far shores barely visible in the distance. The second volcano in this neighborhood, the Osorno, provides us with a point for orientation. The precisely formed cone with its snow-capped peak is incredibly similar to Japan's Mount Fuji and we find ourselves constantly gazing in wonder at this look-alike volcano as we circumnavigate the northern banks of Lago Llanquihue. We are in wide, open countryside, the fields divided by hedges, fences and lines of trees. There are many homesteads surrounded by rich meadows and lush pastures. Rivers meander dreamily through the fertile land and then disappear into the depths of the wide Lago Llanquihue.

Having reached the north shore of the lake, we press on, switching to small country roads that head east, and briefly touching the western tip of Lago Rupanco. A few kilometers further north and we have already reached Puyehue Lake, the eastern end of which lies deep in a mountain valley, which is where we want to go. Verdant meadows push their way into the wide valley; the mountain slopes to the left and right seem far away at first, then draw closer together. Densely wooded hills envelope the road in a casual embrace, forcing it to take evasive action, and finally making it slowly climb upwards. We leave behind the broad fields down in the valley, as dense vegetation has pushed forward almost imperceptibly up to the edge of the road and now things start to get interesting. Previously a leisurely cruise, the road begins to pick up speed. The crumbling, patched asphalt presses ahead determinedly, carving a twisting path higher and higher into dense subtropical rainforest. The atmosphere of this forest is peculiar and memories of other journeys keep flickering through our heads. Our internal compass needle spins in wild

HOTEL / RESTAURANT

LLAO LLAO HOTEL
AV. EZEQUIEL BUSTILLO KM. 25, R8401
SAN CARLOS DE BARILOCHE, RÍO NEGRO
WWW.LLAOLLAO.COM

Asien, Kalifornien, Skandinavien? – Vermutlich müssen wir in einem stillen Moment einfach den Reset-Knopf drücken und dieses turbulente Erlebnis zwischen den Vulkanen der südlichen Anden unter „Parque Nacional Puyehue" abspeichern. Aber dann wirft die „Ruta 215" wieder alles über den Haufen, verblüfft uns mit neuen Eindrücken: Graue, kahle Baumstämme tauchen im Grün des Walds auf, zuerst vereinzelt, dann immer mehr. Irgendwann ähnelt die Umgebung einem dystopischen Albtraum aus toten Bäumen, die mahnend über die weiten Berghänge marschieren, als dürre Geisterarmee. Sind das die Überreste eines lange vergangenen Waldbrands? Die Baumopfer eines Vulkanausbruchs, ausgelöscht von heißen Gasen oder giftiger Asche? – Wir fahren stumm dahin, die Straße schlängelt sich mittlerweile dicht unter den Wolken voran. Blaugraue Knäuel aus dichtem Wasserdampf, an deren drallen Bäuchen die knochigen Ast-Finger von Baumleichen kratzen. Dann sind wir auf der Passhöhe angelangt. Die dort verlaufende Grenze zwischen Chile und Argentinien ist ein kurzer, staubiger Moment, den wir beinahe verpassen.

Plötzlich der Spannung des Aufstiegs beraubt, kurvt die Straße ein paar Augenblicke lang suchend weiter – dann schaut sie in weites Land nach Osten, erinnert sich an ihre Bestimmung und kann es nun plötzlich überhaupt nicht eilig genug haben. Hakenschlagend und Serpentinen-surfend segelt sie dahin, während in der Ferne Berge mit unbekannten Namen den Eingang nach Argentinien bewachen. Mühsam kämpfen wir uns in ihr Reich voran, schlingern durch weite Täler zwischen Granitfelsen, gefüllt mit Farnen, mächtigen Scheinbuchen und Buschwerk. Kahle Bergkuppen bewachen alten Schnee eifersüchtig in Nordrinnen, scheinen den hartnäckigen Ansturm einer kargen Vegetation in hundertjähriger Zeitlupe abzuwehren. Weiter, immer weiter geht es – und dann sind wir plötzlich in einem wahren Märchenland angekommen. Wunderschöne Berge sammeln sich an tiefblauen Seen, urwüchsige Wälder spiegeln sich im Wasser, bunte Blumen bilden neben der Straße opulente Polster. Um aber bis zum Tagesziel in Bariloche zu fahren, müssen wir die

confusion: are we reminded of Asia, California or Scandinavia? – We'll probably just have to hit the reset button in a quiet moment and file this turbulent experience between the volcanoes of the southern Andes under "Parque Nacional Puyehue". But then Route 215 turns everything upside down again, astonishing us with a whole host of new impressions: bare, gray tree trunks appear in the green of the forest, at first sporadically, then more and more frequently. At some point, the environment starts to resemble a dystopian nightmare of dead trees marching threateningly over the wide mountain slopes like a ghostly malnourished army. Are these the remains of a long-forgotten forest fire? Or perhaps the victims of a volcanic eruption, obliterated by hot gases or toxic ash? – We drive on in silence as the road meanders ahead under the low-lying clouds, blue-gray tangles of dense water vapor, the bony fingers of the dead trees scratching their plump underbellies. Suddenly we reach the top of the pass.

We almost miss the border running between Chile and Argentina in a brief, dusty moment. Abruptly deprived of the excitement of the ascent, the road twists on for a short while, casting about to find out what happens next. Then, looking to the wide vistas in the east, it remembers its destiny and suddenly finds itself in a hurry once again. It cruises along, swerving and surfing switchbacks, while in the distance nameless mountains guard the gateway to Argentina. We effortfully carve our way into this domain, lurching through wide valleys between granite rocks, filled with ferns, mighty trees and shrubs. Bald hilltops jealously guard old snow in their north-facing gullies, as if to fend off the stubborn onslaught of sparse vegetation in a slow, hundred-year advance. On and on we go before arriving in a true fairytale land. Beautiful mountains group themselves around deep blue lakes, primeval forests are reflected in the water and colorful flowers form into opulent cushions along the roadside. But in order to reach the destination for today's stage in Bariloche, we need to travel around the lake landscape of Lago Nahuel Huapi in a wide arc – to its eastern foothills and from there

RESTAURANT

LA POSTA PARRILLA PATAGÓNICA
AV. ARRAYANES 263,
Q8407 VILLA LA ANGOSTURA,
NEUQUÉN

CARRETERA AUSTRAL
RIO RAYAS

Beeindruckt rollen wir nach Bariloche hinein, verkriechen uns in der Sicherheit der Stadt und lassen diese ersten Stunden in Patagonien sacken. Die aufwühlende Schönheit der Berge und ihre wilde Vielfalt.

Slightly stunned by the impression gathered, we roll into Bariloche, take shelter in the security of our urban surroundings and let these first hours in Patagonia sink in, contemplating the stirring beauty of the mountains in all their wild diversity.

HOTEL / RESTAURANT

LA CABAÑA FISHING LODGE
RUTA 235, KILÓMETRO 11,
5880000 CHAITÉN, PALENA,
LOS LAGOS
WWW.YELCHOFLYFISHING.COM

Seenlandschaft des Lago Nahuel Huapi in weitem Bogen umrunden – bis an seinen östlichen Ausläufer und dort weiter ans Südufer. Und hier verlieren wir die Berge für einen kurzen Moment. Wir sind am östlichen Fuß der Anden angekommen, schauen fasziniert in die gähnende Weite der argentinischen Pampa, die sich von hier aus viele Hunderte Kilometer nach Osten, vor allem aber Norden und Süden erstreckt. Eine flache Steppe, auf der sich struppige Grasbüschel in Sand und Geröll klammern, während ein stetiger Wind über sie fegt. Scheinbar endlose Dimension, beängstigend in ihrer gleichmäßigen Neutralität.

Beeindruckt rollen wir nach Bariloche hinein, verkriechen uns in der Sicherheit der Stadt und lassen diese ersten Stunden in Patagonien sacken. Die aufwühlende Schönheit der Berge und ihre wilde Vielfalt. Irgendwann treiben wir dann ziellos durch die Stadt. Sind irritiert und amüsiert vom Charakter Bariloches, der Europäern ein sonderbares Gefühl von Altbekanntem gibt, aber auch die sonderbare Stil-Unbekümmertheit so vieler Einwanderer-Städte zur Schau stellt. Im alten Stadtzentrum bilden wuchtige Gebäude eine Art Marktplatz: sie sind aus Granitsteinen gemauert, tragen bullige Türme und winzige Gauben, stützen sich schwer auf Torbögen und Arkadengänge, besitzen teilweise Obergeschosse in Blockhausbauweise. Das könnte so oder ähnlich auch in einem Städtchen der Eifel, im Bergischen Land oder Thüringen, in Süddeutschland, in Tirol oder in der Schweiz anzufinden sein – ein paar Straßen weiter drängen sich dann aber wieder lebhafte Häuserzeilen, die lateinamerikanische Leichtigkeit ausstrahlen. Laute Läden im Erdgeschoss, auf das sich ein niedriges

to the southern shore. Here we leave the mountains behind for a brief moment. We have arrived at the eastern foot of the Andes and are faced with a fascinating view of the yawning expanse of the Argentinian pampas, which stretches from here many hundreds of kilometers to the east, but mainly to the north and south. A flat steppe where tufts of scrubby grass cling to sand and boulders while a never-ending wind sweeps across the land. We find ourselves in a seemingly endless dimension, frightening in its featureless neutrality.

Slightly stunned by the impression gathered, we roll into Bariloche, take shelter in the security of our urban surroundings and let these first hours in Patagonia sink in, contemplating the stirring beauty of the mountains in all their wild diversity. At some point we drift aimlessly through the city. We find ourselves irritated and amused in equal measure by the character of Bariloche, which gives Europeans an uncanny sense of the familiar but also exhibits the oddly stylish insouciance of so many immigrant cities. In the old city center, massive buildings made of granite form a kind of market square, their bulky towers and tiny dormer windows leaning heavily on arched doorways and arcades, some of them with upper floors built in blockhouse style. You could easily find something similar in small town in various German regions from the Eifel and Bergisches Land to Thuringia or Southern Germany and even Tyrol or Switzerland. Just a few streets further on, however, we come across lively rows of houses full of Latin American lightness of spirit. Noisy shops on the ground floor are topped by low residential floors above and brightly colored canopies cover the sidewalk. The mix of architectural styles is confusing, Sankt Moritz meets Santa Fe, old Europe meets new America.

At that moment we decide to abandon all our expectations of Patagonia, Argentina and Chile and simply to embark on the journey. We begin to understand why this corner of the world is known as the "Switzerland of Argentina", but this too leads us down a rabbit hole. Your first instinct is to try to explain the recurring moments in which your synapses start to spark at

CARRETERA AUSTRAL

Wohngeschoss duckt, bis auf den Gehsteig geschobene Überdachungen davor. Das Potpourri der Baustile ist verwirrend, Sankt Moritz trifft Santa Fe, altes Europa trifft neues Amerika. In diesem Moment entschließen wir uns dafür, die Erwartungen an Patagonien, an Argentinien und Chile völlig über Bord zu werfen und uns einfach auf die Reise einzulassen. Wir verstehen nun ja, weshalb dieser Winkel den Titel „Schweiz Argentiniens" trägt, aber er führt auf eine völlig falsche Fährte. Will vermutlich die immer wiederkehrenden Momente erklären, in denen beim Anblick von Bergen und Seen Synapsen zu funken beginnen: Erinnerungen, so unbewusstbewusst wie auf der Zunge liegende Worte. Aber im nächsten Moment ist das verflogen, man nimmt das Fremdartige wahr, den ganz eigenen Charakter des Landes.

Einen Tag später sind wir zurück am Pazifik, fahren zwischen den Vulkanen an den Fjord, vorbei an Puerto Montt und auf die Ruta CH-7 „Carrera Austral" nach Süden. Neben uns zieht die graue Bucht vorbei, im flachen Wasser waten Vögel, der salzigjodhaltige Duft des Schlicks liegt wie ein schwerer Schleier in der Luft. Bei La Arena trägt uns eine Fähre über den Seitenarm des Estero Reloncavi, dann folgen wir der CH-7 weiter nach Süden. Fahren in Gedanken durch Norwegen und Island, zwischen schneebedeckten Anden-Gipfeln und düsteren Fjorden. Genießen die nächste Fährfahrt zwischen Cholgo und Pillan, gute drei Stunden auf stampfendem Schiff, während ringsum ein graugrüner Meeresarm die Sockel der Berge tränkt. So intensiv ist das Hineinschieben des Pazifik ins gebirgige Landesinnere, dass die Straße auch hinter der Mündung des Rio Reñihué keinen Durchgang findet und ein letztes Mal für ein paar Minuten eine weitere Fähre nutzen muss. Erst dann hat die Carretera Austral wieder sicheren Boden unter den Füßen. Tastet sich unterhalb des 2.400 Meter hohen Vulkan Michinmahuida nach Chaitén.

Beim Hineinfahren in die kleine Siedlung spüren wir es: den langsamen Herzschlag der Reise. Wir schwingen in derselben Frequenz wie dieses fremde und gleichzeitig seltsam vertraute Land. Wir sind angekommen. In Patagonien.

Beim Hineinfahren in die kleine Siedlung spüren wir es: den langsamen Herzschlag der Reise. Wir schwingen in derselben Frequenz wie dieses fremde und gleichzeitig seltsam vertraute Land.

As we enter the small settlement we feel the slow pulse of the journey. Our hearts begin to beat at the same frequency as this strange yet oddly familiar land.

the sight of mountains and lakes, evoking memories that are as much part of our subconscious as the words that roll off our tongues. But the next moment that's all gone, as you come to terms with the strangeness, the very unique character of the country.

A day later we are back at the Pacific, cruising between the volcanoes towards the fjords, heading south past Puerto Montt on Route CH-7 "Carrera Austral". A gray-colored bay flashes past us. Birds wade in the shallow water, the salty-iodine scent of the silt hangs in the air like a heavy veil. A ferry at La Arena carries us across the tributary of the Estero Reloncavi, after which we follow the CH-7 further south. Inevitably we are reminded of driving through Norway and Iceland as we weave a path between snow-capped Andes peaks and gloomy fjords. We enjoy the next ferry crossing between Cholgo and Pillan, chugging onwards for a good three hours, while all around the gray-green sea of the inlet washes the bases of the mountains. The Pacific Ocean pushes its way into the mountainous interior so intensely that the road comes to a halt beyond the mouth of the Rio Reñihué and we are forced to take a last ferry for a few minutes. Only then does the Carretera Austral run on solid ground once again, feeling its way forward in the shadow of the 2,400 meter high Michinmahuida volcano to Chaitén.

As we enter the small settlement we feel the slow pulse of the journey. Our hearts begin to beat at the same frequency as this strange yet oddly familiar land. We have arrived in Patagonia.

HOTEL / RESTAURANT

LA CABAÑA FISHING LODGE
RUTA 235, KILÓMETRO 11,
5880000 CHAITÉN, PALENA,
LOS LAGOS
WWW.YELCHOFLYFISHING.COM

PUERTO MONTT CHAITÉN

Mit dem 320-Kilometer-Ausflug über die Anden, hinüber nach Bariloche, setzen wir einen ganz bewussten Auftakt an den Beginn unserer Reise durch Patagonien. Anstatt der „Carretera Austral" nach Süden zu folgen, ziehen wir nach Osten, gegen den Strich der Berge. Auf dem Weg in die „Schweiz Argentiniens" überqueren wir den Anden-Hauptkamm in ganzer Breite und gelangen am östlichen Fuß des Gebirges bis an die weiten Ebenen der argentinischen Pampa. Nicht nur die spannende Fahrt in den Kurven der Nationalparks macht diesen Auftakt-Abstecher für uns zur Pflicht, auch der Besuch Bariloches ist einen Umweg wert. Die Stadt steht beinahe sinnbildlich für die Geschichte Patagoniens: Mit den deutlich wahrnehmbaren Einflüssen deutscher Einwanderer, ihrer Geschichte als ehemaligem Handelsposten im Land der Ureinwohner und der heutigen Leuchtturm-Rolle im Outdoor-Tourismus spiegelt die Departamento-Hauptstadt der Provinz Rio Negro das Werden vieler Städte Patagoniens wider. Zurück am Ausgangspunkt, in Puerto Montt, geht die eigentliche Fahrt nach Süden los – mit einer Etappe entlang der Fjorde am Pazifik. Fährschiffe spielen hier immer wieder eine prägende Rolle, das Déjà-vu für Norwegen-Fans ist unausweichlich.

—

The 320-kilometer journey across the Andes to Bariloche is a very deliberate curtain-raiser to our journey through Patagonia. Instead of following the "Carretera Austral" south, we head east, in the opposite direction to the mountains. On the way to the "Switzerland of Argentina" we cross the entire width of the main Andes ridge, eventually reaching the eastern foot of the mountains and the wide plains of the Argentine pampas. This initial detour is made worthwhile for us not just by the exciting curves as we drive through the national park, but also by the chance to visit Bariloche. The city is almost symbolic of the history of Patagonia: With the clearly perceptible influences of German immigrants, its history as a former trading post among the indigenous populations and its modern flagship role in outdoor tourism, the capital of the Rio Negro province reflects the development of many of Patagonia's cities and towns. Back at our starting point in Puerto Montt, the actual journey south begins with a stage that closely follows the Pacific fjords. Ferries play a formative role, so that a feeling of déjà vu is inevitable for Norway fans.

996 KM • 3 TAGE // 619 MILES • 3 DAYS

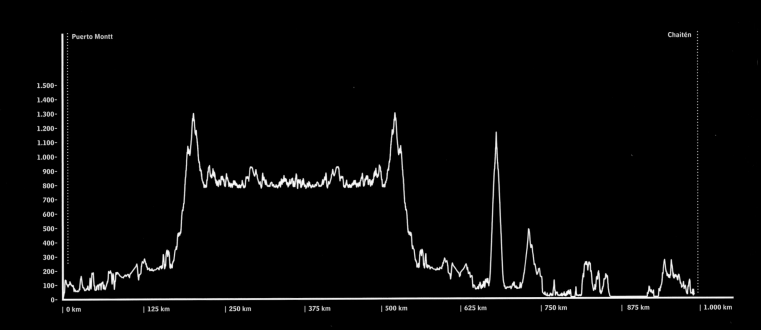

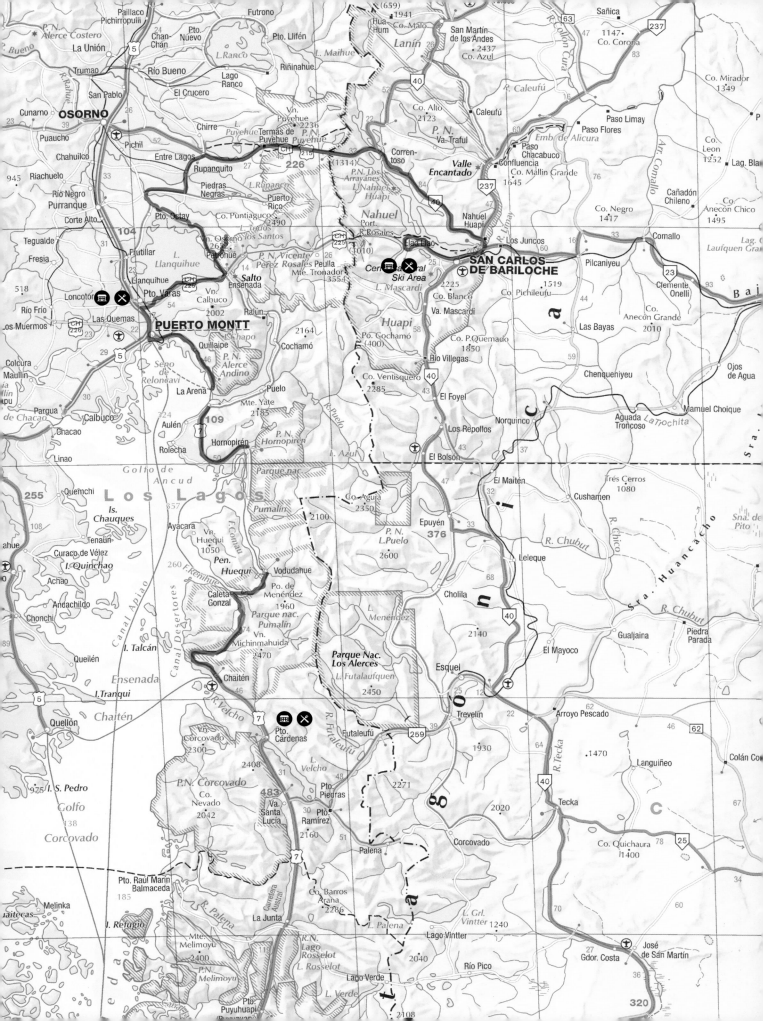

CHAITÉN
COCHRANE

919 KM • 2-3 TAGE // 572 MILES • 2-3 DAYS

Die Anden sind im Westen des Kontinents wie Schwämme. Sammeln Schnee und Eis, saugen sich voll mit Wasser und geben das dann langsam und unaufhörlich wieder dem Pazifik zurück. Rund um Chaitén schieben gleich mehrere Flüsse durch ihr gewundenes Bett, sind Heimat für Forellen und Lachse, schlingern in sattgrünen Tälern dahin.

—

The mountains of the Andes act like a sponge in the west of the South American continent. They gather snow and ice, soaking up water and then gradually and incessantly releasing it back into the Pacific. Around Chaitén, several rivers flow through winding beds, home to trout and salmon, meandering along lush green valleys.

HOTEL

CABAÑAS ROSSBACH
AYSÉN CL, CISNES, AV. OTTO UEBEL S/N,
6010000 PUYUHUAPI, CISNES, AYSÉN
WWW.CABANAS-ROSSBACH.NEGOCIO.SITE

RESTAURANT

RESTAURANT MISUR
PUYUHUAPI, CISNES, AYSÉN

Unten an der Küste verschwinden sie dann ganz unsentimental und ohne jede Abschiedszeremonie im Ozean – übrig bleiben nur Felder aus grauem Geröll und weite Sandbänke: Gestein, von Wetter und Wasser aus den Bergen gebrochen, von den Flüssen in jahrhundertelanger, unermüdlicher Arbeit heruntertransportiert.

Chaitén hat es sich auf einer dieser von Flüssen aufgeschütteten Bänken eingerichtet: Holzhäuser in Schotterstraßen-Quadraten, Schule, Tankstelle, Kirche, Mini-Markt. Vor Holzhütten setzen Kleidungsstücke auf Wäscheleinen die Segel, verwaiste Bolzplätze warten auf Kicker. Ein steter Wind lässt am Pazifik Wellenkronen schäumen, Buschwerk in endloser Unruhe zappeln und tiefliegende Wolken gegen die umliegenden Berge treiben. Zerbeulte Fährschiffe stampfen durch die Bucht und suchen die kleine Autorampe – Hafen kann man diese Landestelle eher nicht nennen. Früher war Chaitén deutlich größer, die Carretera Austral und die Fähren aus Puerto Montt spien globetrottende Outdoor-Nomaden aus. Man strandete hier für ein paar Stunden, machte Verschnaufpause vom Abenteuer oder mietete sich einige Zeit gemütlich in einer der Holzhütten oder Campingplätze ein. – Dann verlor der ein paar Kilometer nördlich gelegene Vulkan Chaitén im Mai 2008 seinen Kopf, bedeckte die Umgebung mit Lava und Asche, schickte eine heiße Lawine aus Schutt und Schlamm bis nach Chaitén. 15 Jahre später kann man die Katastrophe nur noch erahnen, wenn man von ihr weiß. Von den ehemals rund 5.000 Einwohnern der Stadt sind aber gerade einmal etwas über 700 geblieben.

Wir schleichen uns aus der Stadt, Reifen knirschen im Schotter, dann grollt grobes Offroad-Profil auf rauem Asphalt: Kurs Südost, bis ins Tal des Rio Amarillo. Nach einigen kurvigen Kilometern schneidet die CH-7 nun forsch durchs Land, lässt dichte Vegetation links und rechts liegen, macht entschlossen Meter. Eine dichte Decke aus niedrigen Farnen schmiegt sich ringsum ins Gelände, magere Bäumchen sind hier ebenfalls zu finden, bei weitem aber nicht so selbstbewusst: Unschlüssig scheinen sie abwarten zu wollen, ob das raue Klima hier unten für sie ein Auge zudrückt, ob sie bleiben dürfen. Erst an den weiter entfernten Berg-

Down on the coast they then disappear into the ocean unceremoniously and without so much as a backward glance, so all that remains are fields of gray rubble and wide sandbanks: rock split away from the mountains by weather and water to be carried downriver in centuries of tireless effort.

Chaitén has established itself on one of the banks formed by the rivers: wooden houses form squares on loosely graveled roads. There is a school, gas station, church and convenience store. Washing billows on clotheslines in front of small wooden dwellings. Deserted football pitches await the arrival of the players. A constant wind whips up foam on the waves of the Pacific Ocean. Bushes toss about restlessly and low-lying clouds drift by against the backdrop of the surrounding mountains. Battered ferries chug through the bay in search of the small car ramp – this landing spot isn't really enough to be called a harbor. Chaitén used to be much larger when the Carretera Austral and the ferries from Puerto Montt spat out nomadic globetrotting outdoor types. They would be stranded here for a few hours and would take a breather from their adventures or rent comfortable accommodation in one of the wooden huts or campsites for a while. Everything changed in May 2008, when the Chaitén volcano a few kilometers to the north went ballistic, covering the surrounding area with lava and ash and sending a livid avalanche of debris and mud all the way to Chaitén. 15 years later you can only imagine the catastrophe if you know about it. Of the 5,000 or so inhabitants of the town, just over 700 have remained.

We sneak out of town. Our tires crunch in the gravel, then our rough-tough off-road treads rumble on the coarse asphalt: we head southeast, down to the valley of the Rio Amarillo. After a few winding kilometers, the CH-7 now cuts briskly through the countryside, leaving dense vegetation to the left and right, resolute in its progress. A dense blanket of low ferns wraps itself around the area, and there are also slender little trees shyly dotted about: they seem undecided whether to wait and see if the harsh local climate will spare them, allowing them to stay. Forests have only really

CARRETERA AUSTRAL

hängen haben sich Wälder wirklich sesshaft niedergelassen, ein dichter Baumpelz zieht sich hinauf in die Hügel. In der Reihe dahinter ragen schneebedeckte Gipfel auf, der 2.300 Meter hohe Vulkan Corcovado sägt mit spitzem Zahn am eisblauen Firmament: unten ein breiter Kegel, oben ein schroffes Mini-Matterhorn zur Krönung. Sehr charakteristisch, beinahe anmutig, eine wahre Bergschönheit. Und irgendwie hoffen wir nach der Geschichte in Chaitén, dass der Corcovado noch möglichst lange seine Form behält. Wovon man bei den ungemein temperamentvollen Berg-Hitzköpfen dieser Kordilleren-Region leider nicht zwingend ausgehen kann. Letzter Ausbruch des Corcovado: 1835. In Geologie-Zeiträumen also noch nicht so lange her. Was bedeuten kann, dass er es jetzt noch eine kleine Weile ruhig angehen lassen wird. Nochmal 180 Jahre. Oder auch, dass er demnächst mal wieder Druck ablassen wird. Wer weiß das schon, am pazifischen Feuerring.

Wir fahren andächtig und kleinlaut, sehen zu, wie die schneeweißen Gipfel neben uns schweben, nur ganz langsam zurückbleiben. An der nördlichen Spitze des riesigen Lago Yelcho weichen wir mit der CH-7 nach Westen aus, rollen dann auf der Brücke über den Yelcho-Fluss, der hier graugrün wabernd aus dem See watet und oben bei Chaitén im Meer landet. Mürbe Betonpfeiler spannen rostige Hängebrücken-Seile auf, die Fahrbahn ist schmal, kaum breiter als ein Lkw. Wir bleiben einfach stehen, mitten auf der Brücke und schauen: Rechts schlägt sich der Fluss zwischen Sandbänken ins Unterholz, links liegt der See. Schwarzes Wasser unter grauer Wolkendecke, bewaldete Auen waten hinaus, in der Ferne öffnet sich ein weites Tal zwischen majestätischen Bergen. „Déja-vu", funken unsere Gehirne, raunen etwas vom Vierwaldstättersee in der Schweiz, munkeln von den oberitalienischen Seen, erinnern an norwegische Fjorde, flüstern von schottischen Highlands – und die einsam aufragenden Scheinbuchen plappern etwas von „Kenianischem Hochland" dazwischen. Irgendwie haben wir dieses Land immer noch nicht einsortiert, suchen Kategorien und Schubladen. Das muss enden und deshalb geht es weiter. Erfahrungen sammeln beim Fahren. Runter von der Brücke, drei, zwei, eins: Schotter! Seltsam, was das Fehlen

made themselves at home on the more distant mountain slopes, where a dense covering of trees stretches up into the hills. A series of snow-capped peaks rise up, just beyond. The sharp-toothed 2,300 meter high Corcovado volcano gnaws at the ice-blue firmament, a graceful wide cone down below, crowned by a rugged mini-Matterhorn up above. The distinctive shape makes this a true mountain beauty. Somehow, now that we are aware of the story in Chaitén, we hope that the Corcovado will keep itself in check for as long as possible. Unfortunately, this is impossible to predict with the extremely temperamental mountain hotheads of this Cordillera region. The Corcovado last erupted in 1835, which is not that long ago in geological terms. This possibly means it will remain quiet for a little while now. Another 180 years or so... Alternatively, it could let loose any time soon. Anything can happen in the Pacific Ring of Fire.

We make meek and reverent progress, watching as the snow-white peaks float past us, lingering very slowly. At the northern end of huge Lago Yelcho we take the CH-7 to the west, rolling onto the bridge over the Yelcho River, which emerges gray-green from the lake here and ends up in the ocean near Chaitén. Crumbling concrete pillars hold rusty suspension bridge cables in place. The roadway is narrow, barely wider than a truck. We stop in the middle of the bridge and drink in the sights: to the right, the river smashes its way between sandbanks, cutting through the undergrowth, to the left is the lake. The black water spreads itself under a covering of gray cloud.

Tree-filled meadows push outwards and in the distance a wide valley opens up between majestic mountains. A feeling of déjà vu flickers through our brains, murmuring something about Lake Lucerne in Switzerland and the northern Italian lakes, reminding us of Norwegian fjords, whispering in our ears about the Scottish Highlands. In between, the lonely towering trees manage to babble something about the "Kenyan highlands". Somehow we still haven't sorted this country in our heads. We find ourselves looking for categories and pigeon-holes. This needs to come to

HOTEL / RESTAURANT

CABAÑA VALLE EXPLORADORES
PUERTO RÍO TRANQUILO,
LOS ARRAYANES #205,
6060000 AYSÉN, RÍO IBÁÑEZ, AYSÉN
WWW.EXPLORANDOPATAGONIA.CL

CASA BRUJA RESTAURANTE
LOS CHOCHOS 332, PUERTO RÍO
TRANQUILO, RÍO IBÁÑEZ, AYSÉN

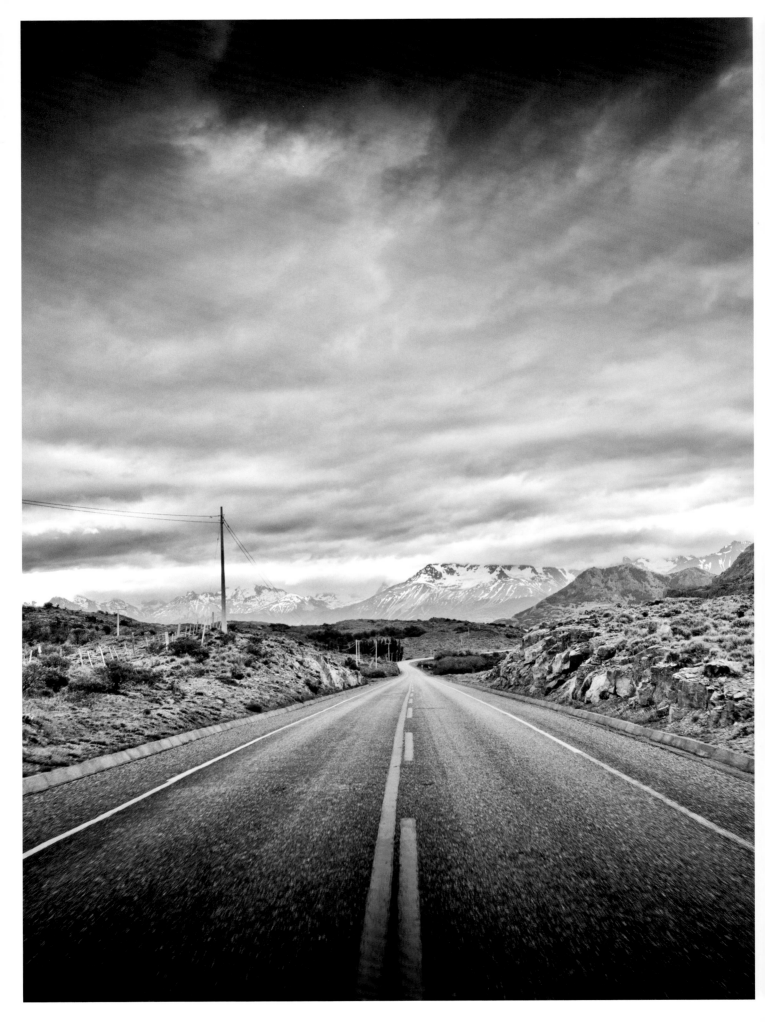

eines Straßenbelags auslösen kann. Schnellerer Herzschlag, weil jetzt das Abenteuer wirklich losgeht. Leise Unsicherheit, weil jetzt die Zivilisation wirklich endet. Freude und Zweifel zugleich. Und so rauschen wir dahin, fühlen uns ein, nehmen das leichte Schwimmen auf dem losen Untergrund prüfend wahr, justieren die Gefühls-Systeme neu. „Schweden", quatscht irgendein Hirnzellen-Reisekommentator dazwischen, weil gerade die braunroten Holzhütten eines Gehöfts am Seeufer vorüberziehen, aber wir hören schon nicht mehr richtig zu. Sind einfach im Jetzt. Führen das Lenkrad gefühlvoll in den Fingerspitzen, spüren den Dialog der Fahrbahn mit den Rädern. Bekommen mit jedem Kilometer ein immer besseres Gefühl für – Schotter. Den ganz feinen mit leichten Spurrillen. Den mit Lehm verschlämmten, der leicht schmiert und rutscht. Den knochentrocken festgewalzten, der sich beinahe so fährt wie eine asphaltierte Straße, wenn da nicht das klackende Prasseln von Rollsplit wäre. Den mittelfesten, der frisch aufgebracht scheint, noch nicht festgefahren, noch nicht zerstört ist. Und dann wäre da tiefer Schotter, aufgerissen von mahlenden Lkw-Reifen, mit tief eingefrästen Spurrillen, die uns schlingern lassen, ganze

an end, which is why we continue to forge ahead. We need to gather experiences as we go. So... it's time to get off the bridge, three, two, one: let's hit the gravel! It's strange what the lack of a paved road can mean. Our hearts beat faster because this is where the real adventure begins. Aware that we have reached the point where civilization ends, we experience a moment of quiet uncertainty, joy and doubt at the same time. And so we push onwards, groping forwards, aware of the slightly floating sensation on the loose substrate, readjusting our senses. Echoes of Sweden pass through our minds as the brown-red wooden buildings of a farmstead on the lake shore flash by, but we're not really listening anymore. We are living completely in the here and now. The steering wheel moves sensitively under our fingertips and we feel the interaction between the road and the wheels, getting a better and better feeling with every kilometer traveled for gravel in its infinite variety. The very fine, slight rutted kind. The muddy kind that slips and slides easily. The bone-dry, compacted kind that feels almost like driving on a paved road if it weren't for the high-pitched patter of loose chippings. The medium-firm kind that seems

Konzentration abverlangen. Haben wir schon die Schlaglöcher, Rinnen und Pfützen erwähnt? Haben wir gesagt, wie viel Spaß dieses Dahinstauben und Vorwärtsmahlen macht? Rallyemomente auf der Carretera Austral. Kilometer um Kilometer. Bis Kilometer keine gültige Währung mehr sind, sondern in etwas großzügigeren Dimensionen gemessen wird.

Hinter Gletschern fahren wir nach Süden, dringen ins Tal des Rio Burritos ein, und als wir im kleinen Ort Santa Lucia mit seinen fünf Querstraßen und drei Längsstraßen landen, macht uns die gellende Stille ohne das Geräusch der Reifen auf Schotter beinahe taub. Viel weiter, bei La Junta – neun Querstraßen, fünf Längsstraßen und eine Flugzeugpiste – biegen wir entlang des Rio Palena nach Westen ab. Zum Meer hin. An der Mündung des Flusses schließen Inseln den Zugang zum Piti-Palena-Fjord ab, hierhin wollen wir. Vielleicht werden auch wir uns eine Weile im langsamen Rhythmus des pazifischen Westens treiben lassen. In den Seen angeln. Auf den Flüssen raften. Delfine beobachten. Mit dem Kayak in die Bucht hinausfahren. Auf Pferden in die Flusstäler hineinreiten, zu heißen Quellen oben im Gebirge, durch feuchten Regenwald. Oder auch einfach nur eine dicke und sämige Muschelsuppe essen. Spaghettidünne frittierte Fische, die beste Freunde von Bratkartoffeln sind. Oder einfach nur mit stetig wachsendem Appetit zusehen, wie ein mächtiger Lachs auf Holzplanken über glühender Kohle gegrillt wird. Dabei saftig und knusprig und ölig wird, während der Duft des schwelenden Holzes sich mit dem Aroma der See vermischt, die gleich neben uns schwappende Wellen auf den Sand wirft. Am nächsten oder übernächsten Tag fahren wir weiter: zurück zur CH-7, die bei La Junta geduldig auf uns gewartet hat, dann in Richtung Süden. Staubend und schotterknirschend, immer weiter. Am Puyuhuapi-Fjord schaltet die bisher schon ungemein eindringliche Natur vollends in den Dramatik-Modus, oben in den Bergen speist der türkisgrüne Eispanzer des Ventisquero-Colgante-Gletschers mit turmhohen Wasserfällen einen milchigen See, der wiederum sein Wasser zum Fjord führt. In einem Seitenarm des Fjords folgt die Carretera Austral schließlich dem Tal des Rio Quelat, immer

like a fresh dressing, not yet bedded in, not yet destroyed. And then there's deep gravel, torn up by grinding truck tires, with deeply milled ruts that make us lurch from side to side, demanding our full concentration. Did we forget to mention the potholes, gullies and puddles? Did we say how much enjoyment can be gained from this type of driving? Rally fever comes to the Carretera Austral! We grind out kilometer after kilometer, until distance no longer has any meaning, but is measured in somewhat larger dimensions.

We head south past glaciers, entering the valley of the Rio Burrito. When we land in the tiny town of Santa Lucia with its five-by-three grid of streets, we are almost deafened by the piercing silence without the sound of tires on gravel. Much further on, at La Junta – a grid of nine-by-five streets and one airstrip – we turn west along the Rio Palena, heading towards the ocean. At the mouth of the river, islands close off access to the Piti-Palena Fjord, which is where we eventually want to go. Maybe we too will let things drift for a while, following the slow rhythm of the Pacific West. Fishing in the lakes. Rafting on the rivers. Watching dolphins. Kayaking out into the bay. Riding horses into the river valleys, to hot springs in the mountains or through humid rainforests. Just relishing a thick and creamy clam chowder or tucking in to spaghetti-like strands of fried fish that go perfectly with fried potatoes. Or simply watching with ever-growing hunger as a huge salmon is grilled on wooden planks over glowing coals. The fish turns juicy, crispy and oily, while the scent of the smoldering wood mixes with the smell of the sea as it casts itself onto the sand right next to us. We continue our journey the next day or the day after, returning to the CH-7 which waits patiently for us at La Junta, then heading south. We press on in a cloud of dust, the crunch of gravel in our ears. At the Puyuhuapi Fjord, Mother Nature cranks up the drama even more. High up in the mountains the turquoise green ice sheet of the Ventisquero Colgante Glacier with towering waterfalls feeds a milky lake, which in turn channels its water to the fjord. In a branch of the fjord, the Carretera Austral finally follows the valley of the Rio Quelat,

HOTEL // HELICOPTER

TERRA LUNA LODGE // HELICOPTER
6050000 PUERTO GUADAL, CHILE CHICO
WWW.TERRALUNA.CL/ES/TERRALUNA-PATAGONIA

HOTEL ULTIMO PARAISO
LAGO BROWN 455, COCHRANE, AYSÉN
WWW.HOTELULTIMOPARAISO.CL

PATAGONIA 47G
SECTOR EL DESAGUE LAGO GENERAL CARRERA - ALDANA, REGIÓN AISÉN DEL GENERAL CARLOS IBÁÑEZ DEL CAMPO

weiter in die Berge hinein. Die Straße wird von der schnellen Piste zum schmalen Pfad, schleicht schüchtern bergauf durchs Dickicht. Große Farnwedel greifen nach dem Auto, eine Art XXL-Rhabarber sammelt Wassertropfen auf riesenhaften Blättern. Dann beißt sich die Straße mit engen Serpentinen in einen Talkessel hinein. Mittlerweile ist die umgebende Vegetation so dicht, dass das schmale Schotterband beinahe überwuchert zu werden droht. Die Fahrt wird immer intensiver, die Landschaft ist wild und überwältigend, ein Gefühl des Ausgesetztseins macht sich breit. Als dann im Tal des Rio Cisnes die Straße vom Schottermodus plötzlich wieder auf Asphalt umstellt, wirkt das regelrecht erleichternd. Zeichen von Zivilisation. Menschengemachte Sicherheit. Die Dosis von Menschenleere bleibt dennoch unfassbar hoch, nur einsame Gehöfte und winzige Weiler sind entlang vieler Kilometer an der Straße zu finden. Bis in die Kleinstadt Villa Mañihuales vergehen Ewigkeiten, rund 90 Kilometer später bietet sich das noch etwas größere Coyhaique als sicherer Hafen bei dieser Entdeckungsreise ins Unbekannte an. Tanken, Essen, Schlafen.

Und dann ändert sich auch langsam, ganz langsam wieder das Land. Schließlich hat uns die CH-7 wieder hinter die Berge verfrachtet, weit weg vom Meer. Der Schatten des Gebirges hält die Wolken zurück, die Welt ist trockener, die Luft glasiger. Milde Steppenmomente mischen sich in die Strenge der südlichen Kordilleren mit ihren Regenwäldern, die Carretera legt aber trotzdem wieder einen Schwenk nach Westen ein. Und hat einen guten Grund dafür: 1.850 Quadratkilometer groß macht sich hier unten der Lago General Carrera breit, drei Viertel seiner Gesamtlänge liegen in den Anden, auf chilenischem Staatsgebiet. Ein Viertel des Sees läuft in Argentinien aus, ist von flacher Pampa-Steppe umgeben – und weil sich die Chilenen und Argentinier immer wieder einmal nicht ganz grün sind, nennt man den See hier drüben auch anders: Lago Buenos Aires. Wir halten uns ganz prinzipiell aus solch strittigen Angelegenheiten heraus, wählen aber für die Umrundung des Sees die chilenische Seite. Natürlich nicht aus einer parteiischen Vorliebe heraus, sondern ganz pragmatisch: Die Carretera Austral zieht im Inneren der Anden nach Süden, wir haben uns an ihre Führungsqualitäten gewohnt und beabsichtigen ihrem Lauf bis zum Ende zu folgen. Am nach Westen, in Richtung Argentinien führenden Abzweig der Ruta 245 halten wir uns deshalb links: CH-7, zurück in die Berge.

In großem Bogen zum Rio Murta, dann wieder an die Sockel der Eisriesen des Laguna-San-Rafael-Nationalparks heran und hier, zwischen Bergen und „General Carrera/Buenos Aires"-See huschen wir nach Süden hindurch. Zu unserer Rechten blecken Gletscher die Zähne, füttern kristallblaue Flüsse und die Straße pflegt wieder einen viele Kilometer währenden Schotter-Moment. Erst hinter dem Ortsschild von Cochrane haben wir wieder festen Boden unter den Füßen.

further and further into the mountains. The road transforms from a fast track to a narrow path, creeping shyly uphill through the thicket. Large grasping fronds of ferns reach for the car, and a species of supersized rhubarb collects drops of water on its gigantic leaves. The road then chews its way into a valley basin in a series of tight serpentines. The surrounding vegetation is now so dense that the narrow strip of gravel is almost in danger of becoming submerged in the undergrowth. The driving becomes more and more intense, the landscape wild and overwhelming. We begin to feel very exposed. It's quite a relief when the road suddenly switches from gravel mode back to asphalt in the valley of the Rio Cisnes. We recognize this man-made safety measure as a sign of civilization. Nonetheless, the level of isolation remains incredibly high, with just the occasional lonely farmstead and tiny hamlet to be found along many kilometers of road. Eternities pass before we reach the small town of Villa Mañihuales. Around 90 kilometers later, the slightly larger settlement of Coyhaique offers a safe haven on this voyage of discovery into the unknown. Time to refuel, eat and sleep.

And then slowly, very slowly, the landscape changes again. The CH-7 has finally taken us back beyond the mountains, far from the coast. The shadow of the mountains holds back the clouds, making the world drier and the air clearer. Mild-mannered steppes mix with the severity of the southern Cordillera and its rain forests, as the Carretera takes another turn toward the west. It has good reason to do so: covering an area of 1,850 square kilometers, Lago General Carrera is a major force down here. Three quarters of its total length is located in the Andes, on Chilean territory. The Argentinian section is surrounded by flat pampas steppe. Because the Chileans and Argentinians do not always see eye to eye, the lake also has a different name on this side: Lago Buenos Aires. As a matter of principle, we don't get involved with such controversial matters, but choose to circumnavigate the lake on the Chilean side. Not out of a partisan preference, of course, but for quite pragmatic reasons: the Carretera Austral heads south within the Andes. We have become accustomed to using the mountains as our guide and intend to follow their course to the end. At the junction with Route 245, which heads west towards Argentina, we keep left, taking the CH-7, back to the mountains.

Making a wide arc to the Rio Murta, we return to the base of the ice giants of the Laguna San Rafael National Park, where we race southwards between the mountains and Lago General Carrera/Buenos Aires. To our right, glaciers bare their teeth, feeding crystal blue rivers and the road becomes a gravel track again for many miles. We only feel solid ground under our feet again after we have passed the sign for Cochrane.

LAGO GENERAL CARRERA

CHAITÉN COCHRANE

Rund 750 Kilometer liegen zwischen Chaitén am Golf von Corcovado und den Gletschergebieten rund um Cochrane, im Süden der Region de Aisén. Wer diese Strecke auf der Carretera Austral befahren möchte, sollte sich auf mehrere Tagesetappen und eine abwechslungsreiche Gangart einstellen. Weite Teile der Strecke sind immer wieder nicht asphaltiert, führen durch menschenleere Gebiete und über anspruchsvolles Terrain. Im Norden wird die Straße von Vulkanen eskortiert, strebt dann vorbei am Corcovado-Nationalpark durch die Región de los Lagosbis zum Puyuhuapi-Fjord, der vom Pazifik her weit ins Landesinnere einschneidet. Hier ändert sich die Richtung der Fernstraße, sie überquert in mehreren Zügen den Anden-Hauptkamm, bis sie bei Coyhaique am östlichen Fuß des Gebirgszugs angelangt ist. Durch die Región de Aysén geht es nun weiter nach Süden, rund um den riesigen Lago General Carrera, der in seinem östlichen, argentinischen Teil „Lago Buenos Aires" genannt wird, dann wieder etwas weiter ins Hochgebirge zurück. In Cochrane haben wir das Ziel unserer Etappe erreicht – und auch beinahe das Ende der Carretera Austral.

—

A distance of around 750 kilometers lies between Chaitén on the Gulf of Corcovado and the glacier fields around Cochrane, in the south of the Aisén region. If you intend to drive this route on the Carretera Austral, you should be prepared for a number of daily stages and a varied pace. Large parts of the route are unpaved and lead through desert areas and across challenging terrain. In the north, the road runs past several volcanoes, then traverses the Corcovado National Park and the Región de los Lagos to reach the Puyuhuapi Fjord, which cuts far inland from the Pacific. The direction of the highway changes here, crossing the main Andes ridge in several stretches until it arrives at Coyhaique at the eastern foot of the mountain range. Passing through the Región de Aysén we continue south, around the huge Lago General Carrera, the eastern, Argentinian part of which is called "Lago Buenos Aires", then head back a little further into the high mountains. In Cochrane we reach the end of this particular stage – and almost the end of the Carretera Austral.

919 KM • 2-3 TAGE // 572 MILES • 2-3 DAYS

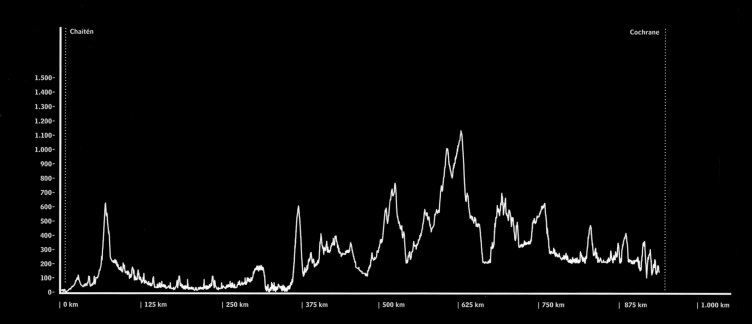

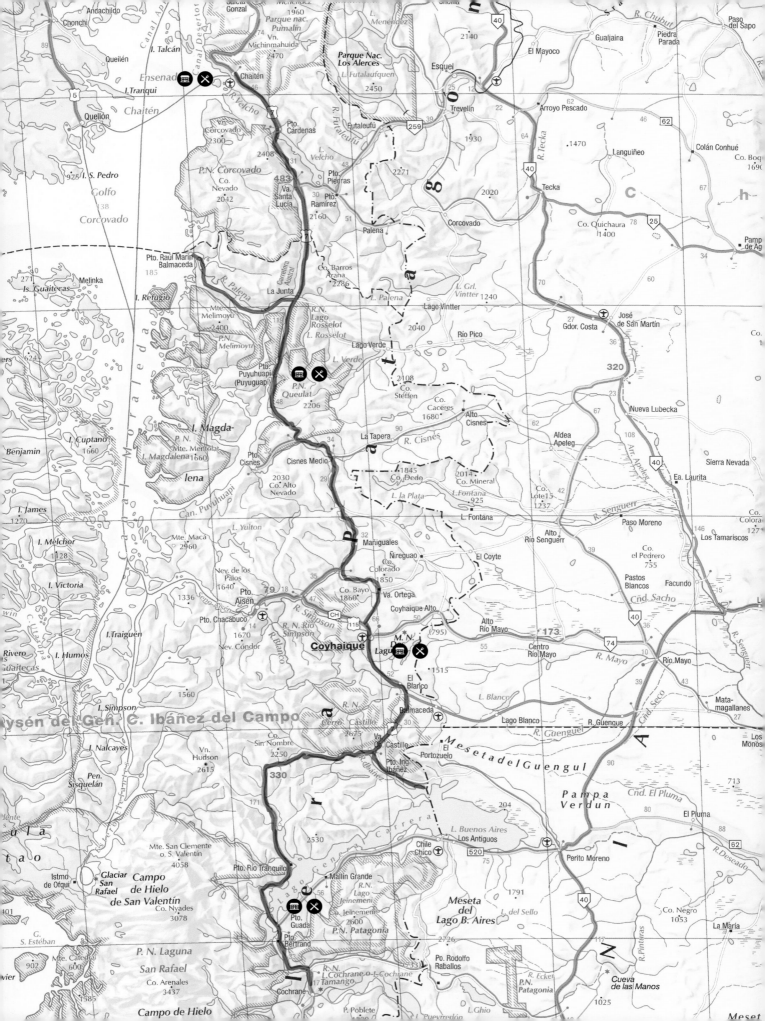

COCHRANE TORRES DEL PAINE

1.700 KM • 5 TAGE // 1.056 MILES • 5 DAYS

Guten Morgen Cochrane. Wir legen uns die Karten für den weiteren Verlauf der Reise. Was heute bedeutet, dass wir uns erst einmal eine Speisekarte legen. Starker Kaffee füllt die Tassen und kreist gewaltig in den Venen, dann landen beeindruckende Teller auf dem Tisch: Mächtige Steaks konkurrieren darauf mit Bratkartoffel-Bergen, Spiegeleier-Pulks machen sich darüber breit.

—

Good morning, Cochrane. We start to lay the plans for how our journey is to continue. First things first: we need to decide what to eat. Strong coffee fills our cups and is already surging powerfully in our veins when impressive plates land on the table: huge steaks compete with mountains of fried potatoes, piles of fried eggs spread out over them.

RESTAURANT

KUSPE
6F4C+42, TORTEL, AYSÉN

Dieser Herausforderung muss natürlich entgegengetreten werden, für die nächsten Minuten herrscht Ruhe. Erst als nur noch magere Reste eines Frühstücks-Gemetzels übrig sind, wird die große Patagonien-Landkarte auf dem Tisch aufgefaltet. Finger laufen entlang von Straßen-Linien nach Süden – und verharren. Zurück zum Ausgangspunkt in Cochrane, neuer Versuch. Irgendwann schauen wir uns an, haben alle dieselbe Überzeugung gewonnen: „Unten in O'Higgins ist Schluss, da geht es für uns nicht weiter." – „Und nochmal ein See, bei dem sich die Chilenen und Argentinier nicht auf einen Namen einigen können ..." – Die Runde grinst, Europäer haben natürlich wenig Verständnis für die Feinheiten der südamerikanischen Völker-Missverständigung. Dass der riesige, bis über 800 Meter tiefe Gletschersee mit seinen vielen Armen auf der chilenischen Seite Lago O'Higgins heißt und in Argentinien Lago San Martin genannt wird, sorgt bei uns Weltreisenden aus einem anderen Universum für Verwirrung. „Die Tehuelche-Ureinwohner sollen den See ja ‚Charre' genannt haben, darauf könnten sich die Chilenen und Argentinier doch wieder einigen", findet ein besonders pfiffiger Kollege –

This challenge must of course be met with determination and for the next few minutes silence reigns. Once the meager remains of breakfast carnage have been cleared away, a large map of Patagonia is unfolded on the table. Fingers run south, following the marked roads – and come to a halt. Back to the start in Cochrane, try again. At some point we look at each other, having all reached the same conclusion: "It's the end of the line down at O'Higgins, we can't go any further." – "Yet another lake for which the Chileans and Argentinians can't agree on a name..." – The group grins, of course Europeans have little understanding for the intricacies of this particular South American stand-off. The fact that the sprawling glacial lake, up to 800 meters deep, is called Lago O'Higgins on the Chilean side and Lago San Martin in Argentina is a source of confusion for us world travelers from another universe. "The Tehuelche natives are said to have called the lake 'Charre', so the Chileans and Argentinians could agree on that," says one particularly clever member of our group – but we don't dare suggest this idea to our Chilean innkeeper for consideration. Who knows what glacial lake-sized diplomatic faux pas

diese Idee unserem chilenischen Gastwirt zur Prüfung vorzustellen, trauen wir uns dann aber doch nicht. Wer weiß, in welches Gletschersee-große Fettnäpfchen wir damit treten würden.

Und wirklich wichtig ist uns eigentlich diese andere Sache: das Ende der CH-7 „Carretera Austral" unten an den Gletschergebieten der Anden. Wir können die Karte auch auf noch so kleine Sträßchen absuchen, die uns hinter O'Higgins nachhaltig weiter nach Süden bringen, werden aber nicht fündig. Im Westen des Anden-Hauptkamms ziehen sich mächtige Fjorde vom Pazifik her bis tief ins Landesinnere, fragmentieren das Festland in Hunderte von Inseln jeder Größenordnung – hier ist kein Durchkommen für eine Straße. Und auch im Osten des Gebirges sieht die Lage kaum anders aus: Ein hunderte Quadratkilometer großer Eispanzer bedeckt das Land, und dort wo er endet, versperren riesige Gletscherseen einen Weg nach Süden. Wer sich in diesem Land bewegen möchte, muss zu Fuß, mit dem Pferd, mit Schiffen oder dem Flugzeug unterwegs sein. Tage- und wochenlang. Für uns bleibt aber nur eine Option: die weite Ausweichbewegung nach Osten. Über die Grenze nach Argentinien, in die Pampa hinein. Bevor wir diesen Weg aber antreten und der Reise damit eine ganz andere Dynamik verleihen, feiern wir einen Abschied von unserer bisherigen Gastgeberin, der Carretera Austral. Etwas über 100 Kilometer wollen wir ihr noch folgen, zuerst hinüber ins Tal des Rio de los Nadis, dann zum Rio Cochrane, der ungefähr 80 Kilometer von der eigentlichen Küstenlinie des Pazifik entfernt bei der kleinen Siedlung Tortel in den Fjord Bajo Pisagua mündet.

Näher als hier kommt man dieser wilden, beinahe unberührten Welt der Fjorde und Inseln an der Westküste Chiles kaum. Das wollen wir sehen. Stauben also über die altbekannte Schotterstraße nach Südwesten, so lang, bis wir dort sind. Am Delta des Rio Cochrane, zwischen mächtigen Bergen, in einer Welt, die neugierig und distanziert auf uns kleine Lebewesen der Spezies Homo sapiens hinabschaut. Wie Figuren einer uralten Vorwelt-Saga kommen wir uns vor, wissen selbst nicht so genau, ob es uns überhaupt gibt, ob wir wichtig sind. Oder doch eher Fabelwesen in einer majestätisch-intensiven, unfassbar realen Natur-Umgebung. Heute hier, morgen verschwunden. Erst der Abend in einer kleinen Kneipe fühlt sich wieder normal an: heimeliges Unterkriechen bei Unseresgleichen, Zusammenrücken gegen die übergroße Naturwelt da draußen. Morchel-Pilze in Sahnesoße auf mehlig gekochten Kartoffelscheiben essen. Oder Sushi, bei dem das Rezept einen Ozean-weiten Weg hinter sich hat, der Fisch aber ultra-frisch ist. Gegrillte Lachsstücke in einer Gemüseterrine. Krabben auf Reis, süßliches Krebsfleisch in knackigem Salat oder Muschelsuppe. Am nächsten Morgen stolpern wir hingerissen von der Szenerie im Tal des Fjords über einen kleinen Holzsteg, der sich rund um Tortel zieht, mit vielen Treppen und Gängen, dann fahren

we'd be making? Anyway, what's really important to us is the other issue: the end of the CH-7 "Carretera Austral" down at the glacier fields of the Andes. Try as we might, we can't find even the narrowest road to take us further south beyond O'Higgins. To the west of the main Andean ridge, mighty fjords cut deep inland from the Pacific, fragmenting the mainland into hundreds of islands of every shape and size so that no road can get through here. The situation to the east of the mountains is not much different: a sheet of ice measuring hundreds of square kilometers covers the country, and where it ends, huge glacial lakes block the way south. If you want to get around in this terrain, you need to travel on foot, on horseback, by boat or by plane. We're talking days and weeks. For us, however, only one option remains: a long evasive maneuver to the east. We need to cross the border to Argentina, entering the pampas.

But before we start out on this path, which will lend our journey a completely different dynamic, we indulge in a celebratory farewell to our previous host, the Carretera Austral. We plan to follow it for a little over 100 kilometers, first across the valley of the Rio de los Nadis, then to the Rio Cochrane, which flows into the Bajo Pisagua Fjord at the small settlement of Tortel, about 80 kilometers from the actual Pacific coast. It is virtually impossible to get any closer to this wild, almost untouched world of fjords and islands on Chile's western coast. This is what we've come to see. We take the familiar gravel road to the southwest to get there. On the delta of the Rio Cochrane, between mighty mountains, we feel like characters from an ancient saga in a world that peers down with curiosity and distance on us tiny examples of the Homo sapiens species. We're not really sure anymore whether we're of any significance or whether we even exist. Maybe we're just mythical creatures in a majestically intense, incredibly real natural environment – here today, gone tomorrow. Things only begin to feel normal again in the evening, when we rub shoulders with our own kind in a small pub, huddled together for protection against the oversized natural world outside. We enjoy morel mushrooms in a creamy sauce on slices of floury potato. Sushi, where the recipe has come from an ocean away, but the fish is super fresh. Grilled pieces of salmon in a vegetable terrine. Shrimp with rice, sweet crab meat in a crispy salad or clam chowder.

The next morning, enthralled by the scenic splendor of the fjord valley, we stumble along the many steps and passageways of the small boardwalk that wraps around Tortel, before returning to Cochrane on the CH-7. This will take us almost a full day again, and because there is still a long distance to go to the Argentinian border in the east, we decide to stay the night. Then, with the first rays of the sun, we head 15 kilometers north to the junction of the X-83 and finally say goodbye to the Carretera. It seems

wir auf der CH-7 nach Cochrane zurück. Auch das wird beinahe wieder einen Tag dauern, und weil es bis zur argentinischen Grenze im Osten noch viele menschenleere Kilometer sind, warten wir die Nacht ab. Ziehen dann mit den ersten Sonnenstrahlen die 15 Kilometer nach Norden zum Abzweig der X-83 und sagen der Carretera hier endgültig Adios.

Dass wir die CH-7 mit ihren langen Schotterpassagen für eine rabiate Begleiterin gehalten haben, scheint uns jetzt lächerlich. Die nach Osten führende X-83 ist kaum mehr als ein Feldweg, gegen sie ist die Carretera Austral tatsächlich eine Schnellstraße mit interkontinentalen Siebenmeilenstiefeln. Unbekümmert, felsig und staubend schnürt die X-83 über die Berge, durchquert weite Täler, die immer trockener werden und die alpinen Momente der hinter uns liegenden Anden vergessen lassen. Legionen von kleinen Gasbüscheln beugen sich neben der Piste wie die Zelte von Kobolden in die Steppe. Holzige Kleinststräucher mit bunten Mini-Blüten heften sich an Felsen und ins Geröll. Lupinen warten am Straßenrand in kleinen Grüppchen auf einen Bus, der niemals kommen wird. In weiter Ferne zeigen sich dunkle Berge mit Kronen aus altem Firnschnee.

Die Grenze zwischen Chile und Argentinien liegt auf einem Felsplateau am „Rodolfo Roballos"-Pass, die Szenerie ist atemberaubend: stahlblauer Himmel, über den majestätische Cirruswolken federn, leuchtend bunte Felsen, grünes Gestrüpp und in der Ferne brachiale Bergriesen mit mächtigen Eiswänden. Auf der argentinischen Seite ändert die Straße ihren Namen, stürzt sich als RP41 in Richtung Westen. Wir lassen den groben Schotter der Piste nur so fliegen, surfen durch versteckte Täler und weite Wüstenareale, bis wir irgendwann auf der von Norden heransegelnden RN40 gelandet sind. Die hat bereits den weiten Weg aus Bariloche herunter in den Beinen, war dahinter aber auch noch viel weiter unterwegs: Aus dem Norden Argentiniens kommt sie, abgekämpft, staubig und routiniert. Das Prasseln des Schotters verebbt schlagartig und dann ist da nur das beruhigende Summen der Reifen auf glattem Asphalt. Beinahe traumwandlerisch fegt die

ridiculous to us now that we regarded the CH-7, with its long stretches of gravel, as a rough traveling companion. The eastbound X-83 is little more than a dirt track, making the Carretera Austral seem like a superfast intercontinental expressway. Without a care in the world, the X-83 snakes its way over the mountains and crosses wide valleys that get increasingly drier, making us forget the alpine terrain of the Andes we have left behind. Small tufts of grass huddle beside the track like legions of goblins' tents in the steppe. Little woody shrubs with tiny colorful flowers cling to rocks and scree. Tight groups of lupins wait patiently at the side of the road for a bus that will never come. Dark mountains capped with old firn snow can be seen in the far distance.

The border between Chile and Argentina coincides with a rocky plateau at the "Rodolfo Roballos" pass. The scenery here is breathtaking: steel-blue sky swathed in majestic, fast-moving cirrus clouds, brightly colored rocks, green scrub and, in the distance, brutal mountain giants with mighty ice walls. On the Argentinian side, the road changes name, tumbling west as the RP41. We send the rough gravel flying as we surf through hidden valleys and wide desert areas until we eventually land on the RN40 as it sails in from the north. Dusty and tired-looking, it has come a long way down from Bariloche, having already covered many miles before that, originating in northern Argentina.

The noise of the gravel dies down abruptly and then there's just the soothing hum of the tires on smooth tarmac. Almost in a dreamlike state, the RN40 sweeps south, sometimes in wide curves, often just straight as a die. This goes on for hours, but feels like endless years. Then, at some point, when we're least expecting it, we find we have reached the eastern end of Lago Viedma. We turn right and drive along the north shore of the lake towards the mountains. Full of anticipation, we keep our eyes straight ahead and wait. A narrow band of snow-covered mountains appears in front of us, first as individual peaks, then connecting to form a chain across the entire horizon. The mountains grow slowly. They

HOTELS

ESTANCIA LA QUINTA
RUTA 23 KM 85
9301 EL CHALTÉN PCIA DE SANTA CRUZ
WWW.ESTANCIALAQUINTA.COM.AR/EN
....

RESTAURANT

PARRILLA LA OVEJA NEGRA
EL CHALTÉN, SANTA CRUZ PROVINCE
....

FITZ ROY

PERITO-MORENO-
GLETSCHER

RN40 nach Süden, manchmal in weiten Bögen, oft auch einfach nur schnurgeradeaus. Stundenlang. Gefühlt jahrelang. Gefühlt endlos. Und dann, irgendwann, als wir beinahe schon nicht mehr daran glauben, haben wir das östliche Ende des Lago Viedma erreicht. Biegen nach rechts ab, fahren am Nordufer des Sees entlang in Richtung der Berge. Wir schauen gespannt geradeaus und warten. Vor uns taucht das schmale Band eines schneebedeckten Gebirges auf, zuerst sind einzelne Gipfel zu sehen, dann verbinden die sich zu einer Kette über den ganzen Horizont hinweg. Langsam wächst das Gebirge in die Höhe. So hoch, bis man irgendwann den Atem anhält, weil da vorne brachiale, zornige Zinnen aufragen. 3.400 und 3.100 Meter aus purem Granit, Reißzähne in die Troposphäre, Fitz Roy und Cerro Torre heißen diese Berge. Klick, macht es im Kopf, wenn deine Synapsen ein Erinnerungsfoto für die Ewigkeit schießen und es in deinem Gehirnwohnzimmer an die Wand pinnen. Klick. Der Wahnsinn. Dass Berge anschauen ein spirituelles Erlebnis sein kann, haben wir geahnt – jetzt wissen wir es ganz sicher.

Die Gänsehaut reicht noch den ganzen, langen Weg zurück zur RN40 und die vielen Kilometer bis zum Lago Argentino, der südlich des Viedma-Sees aus den Anden heraus in die Pampa hinaus strebt. Vier, fast fünf Stunden lang ist dieser Weg, den wir mit euphorischen Gefühlen geladen antreten. Die Granitberge im vergletscherten Süden der Anden geben einem das Gefühl, eine Audienz bei Göttern zu haben. Ihre bedrohliche, gewalttätige Schönheit ist unbeschreiblich. Nur langsam tritt das in uns abgelagerte Gefühl ihrer Erhabenheit zurück, die eintönige Straße nach Süden fordert emotionalen Tribut. Nutzt ab, holt uns in die Realität zurück. Hinein. In. Jeden. Einzelnen. Kilometer. Wir fahren. Und fahren. Oder schiebt sich ringsum einfach ein Neutrum aus beigem Geröll rückwärts? Irgendwann haben wir alle Gespräche geführt, alle Gedanken gedacht. Sind einfach still. Leben im gleichmäßigen Summen des Motors, im gleichmäßigen Schnurren der Reifen auf dem Asphalt.

Als dann plötzlich doch unser nächster Abzweig erreicht ist, einfach so, ganz banal, ist das wie ein Schock. Aber wir sind ganz

Langsam wächst das Gebirge in die Höhe. So hoch, bis man irgendwann den Atem anhält, weil da vorne brachiale, zornige Zinnen aufragen. 3.400 und 3.100 Meter aus purem Granit, Reißzähne in die Troposphäre, Fitz Roy und Cerro Torre heißen diese Berge.

The mountains grow slowly. They reach such a height that at some point you draw breath in awe at the violent, angry battlements towering before you. 3,400 and 3,100 meters of pure granite pierce the troposphere – the Fitz Roy and Cerro Torre.

reach such a height that at some point you draw breath in awe at the violent, angry battlements towering before you. 3,400 and 3,100 meters of pure granite pierce the troposphere – the Fitz Roy and Cerro Torre. You feel something go click inside your head as your synapses take a souvenir snapshot for eternity and pin it to the photo-wall somewhere in your brain. What madness. We always suspected that gazing at mountains could be a spiritual experience – now we know for sure.

We continue to feel goosebumps all the way back to the RN40 and during the long journey to Lago Argentino, which stretches out of the Andes and into the pampas south of Lake Viedma. Embarking on this route in a euphoric state, we drive on for close to five hours. The granite mountains in the glaciated south of the Andes make you feel like you're communing with the gods. Their menacing, violent beauty is indescribable. We slowly begin to feel less in awe of their grandeur as the monotonous road to the south takes an emotional toll. It wears us out and hauls us back to reality. Over... every... single... kilometer. We drive on and on. Or could it be that we are completely stationary while a backdrop of beige rubble pushes past all around us? At some point we all engaged in conversation. We all had thoughts. Now we are just silent, experiencing life through the steady hum of the engine and the monotonous purr of the tires on the asphalt.

It comes as a shock when we suddenly come upon our next junction, just like that in

HOTEL

LAS DUNAS HOTEL
AV. COSTANERA NESTOR KIRCHNER 751,
EL CALAFATE,
SANTA CRUZ
WWW.LASDUNAS.COM.AR

RESTAURANT

LA TABLITA
CNEL. ROSALES 28, EL CALAFATE,
SANTA CRUZ.
WWW.LA-TABLITA.COM

schnell zurück in der Gegenwart. Auch hier unten wollen wir die Hauptstraße noch einmal verlassen. Im Süden des Lago Argentino marschiert nämlich wieder ein schmales Asphaltband zum Fuß der Anden, umrundet eine große Halbinsel und entlarvt dann, dass sich der Argentino-See hier hinten viele Neben-Arme hat wachsen lassen: milchiggraublaues Wasser zwischen wild aufragenden Bergen. Und ganz vorn schiebt sich der Perito-Moreno-Gletscher heran, reißt ein grausames Maul auf, erbricht leuchtende, türkisblaue Eisbrocken in den See. Was für ein Anblick. Klick. Unvergessen.

Bei der weiteren Fahrt nach Süden diskutieren wir: Dass die Gletscherriesen der Erde für künftige Generationen vielleicht nur noch Foto-Erinnerungen sein sollen, bedrückt uns. In den europäischen Alpen sind manche Gletscher vollkommen verschwunden, andere nur noch ein Schatten ihrer früheren Größe, und selbst die so unantastbar wirkenden Gletscher Patagoniens sollen trotz ihrer geografischen Nähe zum Eis der Antarktis in den letzten Jahrzehnten bereits dreißig Prozent verloren haben. Das Eis verschwindet langsam, aber stetig. Nachdenklich fahren wir weitem Bogen in die Pampa hinaus, rollen dann durch eine hügelige Mondlandschaft nach Süden. Immer wieder streift die RN40 ihre zivilisierte Asphaltschicht ab und ist dann kilometerweit „oben ohne" unterwegs: Wir rumoren auf einer dünnen Schotterdecke dahin, die Piste wird zur reinen Empfehlung. Dann ist plötzlich der Asphalt zurück, aber in allen Richtungen kein Land in Sicht, der Horizont lediglich eine Ahnung von Erdkrümmung. Rund 280 Kilometer haben wir seit dem Moreno-Gletscher zurückgelegt, dann sind wir am vorletzten Navigationspunkt der Etappe angelangt: dem Abzweig in Richtung Torres del Paine. Drüben in Chile warten die Berge. Über den Pass am Rio Don Guillermo wechseln wir das Land, warten ein paar Minuten zwischen den Hütten der Grenzbeamten auf Abfertigung und Kontrolle, während ein kalter Wind alles in Deckung gehen lässt. Polarluft, denken wir.

Und dieser kalte Wind weht uns hinein nach Torres del Paine, einen Ort in der Pampa, zwischen kahlen Hügeln. Das Ziel unserer Etappe. Einen Moment lang durchatmen zwischen Naturwundern.

quite a banal moment. We find ourselves back in the present very quickly. Here too our instinct is to leave the main road again. South of Lago Argentino, a narrow strip of asphalt proceeds to the foot of the Andes, circumnavigates a large peninsula and then reveals that Lago Argentino has grown many side arms back here: milky-grey-blue water presses between wild, towering mountains. Right in front, the Perito Moreno Glacier pushes forward, opens its cruel maw and spews shining, turquoise-blue chunks of ice into the lake.

What a sight. Click. Unforgettable. As we continue our journey south we get deep into discussion: we are depressed by the thought that the glacier giants of the earth might perhaps only be photo memories for future generations. In the European Alps, some glaciers have already completely disappeared, while others are only a shadow of their former selves, and even the seemingly untouchable glaciers of Patagonia are said to have already lost thirty percent of their mass in recent decades, despite their geographical proximity to the Antarctic ice. The ice is slowly but steadily disappearing.

Wrapped in thought, we drive in a wide arc into the pampas, then head south through a hilly lunar landscape. The RN40 repeatedly sheds its civilized layer of asphalt and goes "topless" for miles: we rumble along on a thin layer of gravel and the road becomes more like a suggested path than a fixed route. Then suddenly the asphalt returns, but there is no land in sight in any direction and the horizon is just a clue to the curvature of the earth. We have covered around 280 kilometers since the Moreno Glacier when we arrive at the penultimate way point on this stage of our journey: the turn for Torres del Paine. Over in Chile the mountains await us. We cross the border on the pass at the Rio Don Guillermo, wait a few minutes between the border guards' huts for clearance and customs checks, while a cold wind drives everyone to take shelter. Polar air, we assume.

This cold wind blows us into Torres del Paine, a place in the pampas between bare hills. This is our final destination on this stage. We take a deep breath and drink in the natural wonders.

COCHRANE TORRES DEL PAINE

Lago Argentino, Lago Viedma und Lago O'Higgins/Lago San Martin: Diese drei gewaltigen Gletscherseen sind die Speicher des Schmelzwassers einer riesigen Eiskappe über den Anden. Und sie machen sich direkt auf unserer Route von Nord nach Süd breit, lassen kein Durchkommen. Dabei sind sie allesamt von betörender Naturschönheit, einfach Vorbeifahren beinahe unmöglich. Unsere Route geht deshalb pragmatisch vor: Nach einem Besuch der Fjordlandschaft rund um die Bajo Pisagua fahren wir auf der Carretera Austral in Richtung Norden, dann Osten, überqueren die Grenze nach Argentinien und rollen dann in der weiten Pampa nach Süden. Auf dieser Umgehungsroute ist enormes Sitzfleisch notwendig, die nahezu endlos wirkenden Kilometer auf den Straßen durch die südamerikanische Hochlandsteppe können zermürbend sein. Allerdings ist von dieser Seite des Gebirges her ein guter Zugang zu den atemberaubenden Schönheiten Patagoniens möglich: den Bergen Fitz Roy und Cerro Torre westlich von El Chaitén, sowie den Gletschern in den Seitenarmen des Lago Argentino. Und während sich diese spektakulären Sehenswürdigkeiten in unseren Reise-Erinnerungen fest einnisten, schaffen das am Ende auch die Kilometer durch die Pampa: Als magisches Gefühl, als Ahnung von ungeheurer Weite. Stetige Fortbewegung im gemächlichen Rhythmus der Langstrecke. Auch das hat einen meditativen Reiz. Das Ziel unserer Etappe liegt in Torres del Paine – einem unscheinbaren Ort zwischen Pampa und Bergen, aber wieder am Tor zu einem Wunder Patagoniens.

—

Lago Argentino, Lago Viedma and Lago O'Higgins/Lago San Martin: these three mighty glacial lakes are the reservoirs of meltwater from a huge ice cap that covers the Andes. And they spread out directly on our route from north to south, blocking our path. Each one of them is of beguiling natural beauty, making it almost impossible to just drive past. Our route therefore involves a pragmatic approach: after a visit to the fjord landscape around Bajo Pisagua, we head north on the Carretera Austral, then east, cross the border into Argentina and then roll south through the wide pampas. Enormous patience is required on this bypass route, as the seemingly endless distances on the roads through the South American highland steppes can be grueling. However, this side of the mountain range offers plenty of access to the breathtaking beauties of Patagonia: the Fitz Roy and Cerro Torre mountains west of El Chaitén, as well as the glaciers in the side arms of Lago Argentino. While these spectacular sights are firmly embedded in our travel memories, the distance traveled through the pampas also plays its part in the end: a magical feeling, an impression of immense vastness. Continuous steady movement in the leisurely rhythm of long-haul travel also has a meditative appeal. The final destination of this stage is in Torres del Paine – an unremarkable spot between the pampas and the mountain, but yet another gateway to the wonders of Patagonia.

1.700 KM • 5 TAGE // 1.056 MILES • 5 DAYS

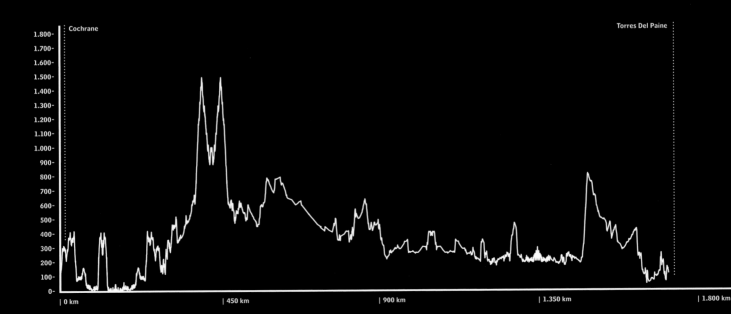

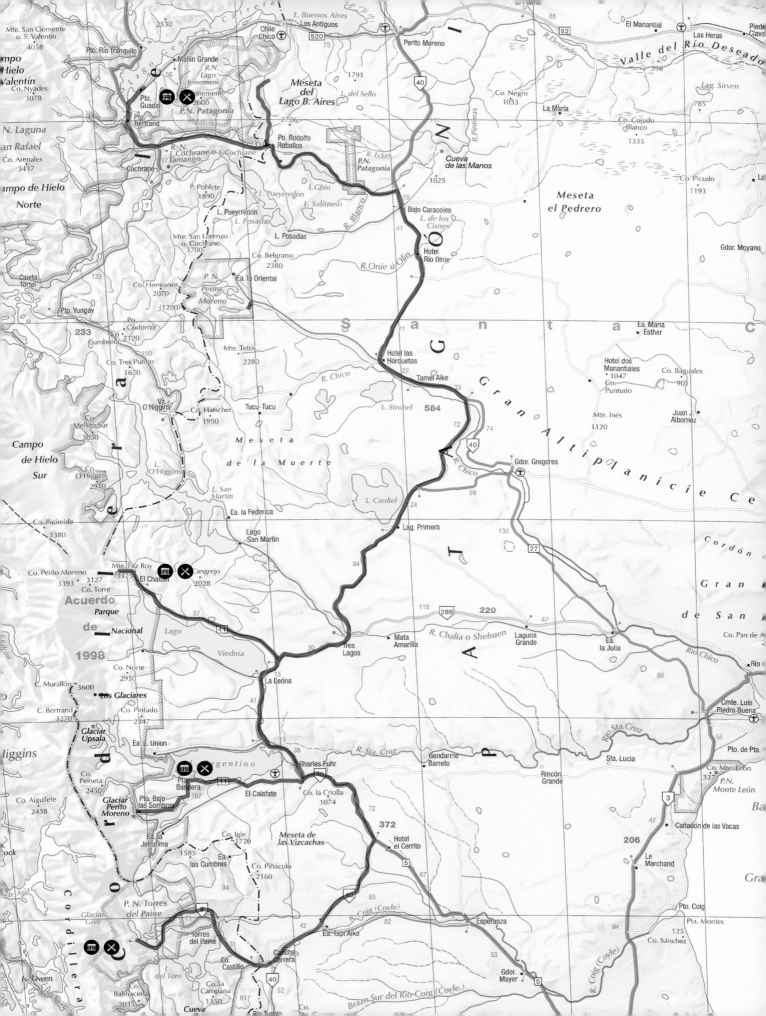

TORRES DEL PAINE USHUAIA

1.022 KM • 2-3 TAGE // 635 MILES • 2-3 DAYS

Türme des blauen Himmels. Wenn man vor ihnen steht, weiß man sofort, weshalb die Tehuelche-Ureinwohner Patagoniens diese Berge so nannten. Schroffe Felsnadeln, die einen stahlblauen Himmel durchpflügen, sich auf brutale Granitsockel pflanzen und in Eiswasser-Seen gründen. Gesättigt mit Farben sind sie, Grau, Ocker, Orangerot, Elfenbein, Silber, und strahlend weiß.

—

When you stand in front of these mountains, you immediately understand why the native Tehuelche people of Patagonia referred to them as blue sky towers. The rugged pinnacles pierce the steel-blue sky, planting themselves on brutal granite plinths and plumbing the depths of icewater lakes. They are saturated with colors – gray, ocher, orange-red, ivory, silver, and brilliant white.

HOTEL

HOTEL LAS TORRES PATAGONIA
ESTANCIA CERRO PAINE S/N, 6170000
TORRES DEL PAINE
WWW.LASTORRES.COM

TIERRA PATAGONIA HOTEL & SPA
ON THE EDGE OF TORRES DEL PAINE
NATIONAL PARK, TORRES DEL PAINE
WWW.TIERRAHOTELS.COM

Die Strahlen der aufgehenden Sonne machen sie zu überirdisch leuchtenden Raumschiffen, gerade gelandet und dampfend vom Flug durchs All. Selbst die Umgebung dieser Titanen ist großartig, atemberaubend schön und regelrecht mythisch. Bis zu 3.000 Meter hohe Berge bevölkern den Nationalpark der Torres del Paine, knirschende Gletscher schieben sich zwischen ihnen hindurch. Weit ins Land geschnittene Fjorde und große Seen nehmen Raum ein, ausgedehnte Wälder von Südbuchen, immergrünen Olivillo-Bäumen und struppigen Zypressen machen sich breit, moorige Tundra-Wiesen füllen die Landschaft mit ihrer bunten Vielfalt.

Ganze Busladungen von Touristen werden aus dem 140 Kilometer weiter südlich gelegenen Puerto Natales herangefahren, die dann zuerst schnatternd und zunehmend selig Gäste in einem Land sind, das keinen kalt lässt. Und auch wir lassen uns treiben: Besteigen die Berge, ziehen auf schmalen Pfaden durchs Land, bestaunen das Kalben der Gletscher. Weiterfahren ist erst einmal keine Option, käme uns wie eine Verschwendung dieser Schönheit um uns herum vor. Die Vorstellung, Patagonien am Ende dieser Etappe verlassen zu müssen, erscheint uns auf einmal unwirklich und verletzend. Weshalb sollte man hier wieder wegwollen? Zurück in eine Welt der Städte, der Menschen, der Geschwindigkeit, der überflüssigen Informationen, der vermeintlichen Dringlichkeiten? In der Algorithmen Gewohnheiten tracken und dem tumben Konsum-Neandertaler in uns (Moment mal, waren die vielleicht sogar klüger als wir?) persönlich zugeschnittene Angebote zum Lebenszeit-Diebstahl unterbreiten? – Kauf dies, kauf das. Klick hier, klick da. Reg dich auf, reg dich ab.

Wenn man aber auf einem Felsen am Ufer des Lago Grey sitzt, während ein kalter Polarwind die Blättchen der kleinen Sträucher wirbeln lässt und die weite Oberfläche aus graublauem Gletscherwasser in eine Richtung bürstet – blinkend, glitzernd, stetige Bewegung im Verharren des Wassers und der doch so fest verwurzelten Pflanzen – dann treten die Zeit-Staubsauger zurück. Das Mobiltelefon in deiner Tasche ist nun weder smart noch Phone, denn null Balken auf

The rays of the rising sun transform them into unearthly glowing spaceships, newly landed and steaming from their flight through space. The landscape surrounding these titans is equally magnificent, breathtakingly beautiful and the stuff of legend. Mountains measuring up to 3,000 meters in height populate the Torres del Paine National Park, interspersed with creaking, crunching glaciers pushing their way between them. Fords make deep incisions inland and large lakes spread themselves extravagantly and broad swathes of native trees – beech, evergreen olivillo and cypress – make a daring land grab. Vast areas of boggy tundra fill the landscape with brightly colored vegetation of every variety.

Whole bus-loads of tourists are disgorged here after a 140-kilometer journey from Puerto Natales down south. These chattering hoards become increasingly serene as they spend more time in a country that leaves no one cold. We have caught the bug too: we climb the mountains, follow narrow tracks through the countryside, gaze in awe as the glaciers split and sunder. An immediate resumption of our journey is not an option, as it would be a waste of the enormous beauty that surrounds us. The idea of leaving Patagonia at the end of this stage seems unimaginable and quite painful right now. Why on earth would you want to leave this place? Who would wish to return to a world full of cities and people, speed, information overload and a spurious sense of urgency? Why return to the familiar algorithm-based patterns that appeal to the dumb consumerist Neanderthal in all of us? (Maybe the Neanderthals were smarter than us after all.) Why fall prey to the personalized advertising that simply causes us to fritter away our precious lifetime? – Buy this, buy that. Click here, click there. Go faster, slow down.

But it feels like time stands still when you sit on a rock on the shores of Lago Grey while a cold polar wind whips the leaves of the small shrubs and combs the wide surface of grey-blue glacial water in a single direction, producing glittering flashes of constant movement on the surface of the still water and among the leaves of the firmly rooted plants. The phone in your pocket is now not that smart anymore, because zero bars on

dem Display legen es still. Am Abend, wenn der Akku leer ist, wird nicht einmal mehr das Fotografieren gehen, dann ist der Apparat vollends nutzlos, du wirst kaum einen Nagel damit einschlagen können. Aber hey, es ist dir gerade sowieso egal, wo irgendwelche Aktien stehen, welche Mannschaft im Soundso-Cup führt, welcher Trend gerade nur deine Seele will.

Neben dir sitzt ein lieber Mensch, hat das Kinn auf die angezogenen Knie gelegt und blinzelt in die Sonne. So sieht Glücklichsein aus. Du schaust hinüber und willst gerade deinen Mund öffnen, ihn in all die Erkenntnisse einweihen, die dir gerade eine Gänsehaut bereiten, dich dem Sinn des Universums und des Lebens näherbringen – da fällt dir auf, dass auch diese Seele neben dir gerade einfach nur hier ist. Sie wird das alles schon selbst merken, früher oder später, ganz bestimmt – oder vielleicht bist du ja bereits der Letzte, der all das spürt und die anderen sagen nur einfach nichts, haben auf dich gewartet ...? In genau dieser Sekunde dreht sich die Erde mit 1.670 km/h um ihre eigene Achse, rast 108.000 km/h schnell auf ihrer Bahn um die Sonne, wirbelt samt unserem ganzen Sonnensystem mit 792.000 km/h ums Zentrum der Galaxie. Hast du irgendwo gelesen. Und wunderst dich, dass dir das gerade jetzt einfällt. Vielleicht wegen allem, was gerade in dieser Sekunde auf dieser Welt geschieht. Unfassbares Glück, entsetzlicher Schmerz, alles überwindende Liebe, zerfetzender Hass. Und unser Planet fliegt einfach vor sich hin. Unser Herz schlägt. Einatmen, ausatmen. Wir existieren. „Jetzt merkst du es auch", lächeln die Blüten auf dem Heidekraut und die Flechten auf den Felsen, „wie gut es ist, da zu sein".

Auf der Piste nach Süden oberhalb des Lago el Toro nabeln wir uns von Torres del Paine ab. Schauen wehmütig zurück, haben aber auch wieder genug Fernweh gesammelt, um die vielen Meilen vor uns mit Neugier anzugehen. Berge stehen Spalier und begleiten uns auf dem Weg: ausladende Riffe aus grauem Fels, mächtige Gebirgsstöcke und schneebedeckte Zinnen. Kurz bevor die Straße aus dem Nationalpark hinaus auf die nach Süden führende Ruta 9 trifft, prescht plötzlich ein Rudel Guanakos über die Straße. Mit steifem Hals und eckigen Bewegungen überqueren sie die Fahrbahn, bremsen uns aus. Gerade, als ob sie uns auf etwas aufmerksam machen wollten. Und dann haben wir auch schon den Grund für einen Stopp: Links der Straße, keine hundert Meter entfernt, öffnen sich gigantische

the display mean it is almost pointless. In the evening, when the battery is empty, you won't even be able to take pictures, making the device completely useless. You couldn't even use it to hammer a nail home. But hey, who cares about the stock markets, or which team is winning in whatever league, or even which new trends your soul should be crying out for.

A friend is sitting next to you, his chin on his knees, squinting at the sun. This is what happiness looks like. You look over and are just about to open your mouth to share all the insights that are giving you goosebumps, bringing you closer to the meaning of the universe and life when you realize that this person next to you is also having a similar experience. He will definitely notice all this for himself, sooner or later. In fact it is quite possible that you may be the last person to experience this feeling and the others just haven't said anything because they were waiting for you to catch up. At this precise moment, the earth is rotating on its own axis at 1,670 km/h, racing at 108,000 km/h on its orbit around the sun, and our entire solar system is whirling around the center of the galaxy at 792,000 km/h. You're sure you read that somewhere. You're also surprised to find yourself thinking about that right now. Maybe it's because of everything that's happening in this world right this second. Incredible happiness, excruciating pain, all-conquering love, excoriating hatred. And our planet simply keeps turning. Our hearts keep beating. Breathe in, breathe out. We exist. "Now you've got the message too," smile the blossoms on the heather and the lichen on the rocks. "You know how good it is to be alive."

On the road to the south above Lago el Toro we turn away from Torres del Paine. We look back wistfully, but also muster enough wanderlust to tackle the many miles ahead with curiosity. Mountains stand to attention and guide us on our way: hulking reefs of gray rock, mighty mountain ranges and snow-capped peaks. Just before the road leading out of the national park meets the southbound Route 9, a pack of guanacos suddenly dashes across our path. With stiff-necked, angular movements, they cross in front of us and slow us down. It's almost as if they wanted to draw our attention to something. We quickly find a reason to stop: to the left along the road, less than a hundred meters away, gigantic caves open under the towering mountain, the Cuevas del Milodón. The water from primeval

Y-635

HOTEL

HOTEL ALTIPLANICO SUR
HUERTOS FAMILIARES 282 NATALES,
6160000 MAGALLANES
WWW.ALTIPLANICO.CL/ALTIPLANICO-
PUERTO-NATALES/

THE SINGULAR PATAGONIA, PUERTO
BORIES HOTEL
KM 5, 5 NORTE S/N, 6160000 NATALES,
MAGALLANES Y LA ANTÁRTICA CHILENA
WWW.THESINGULAR.COM

Höhlen unter dem hier aufragenden Berg, die Cuevas del Milodón. Das Wasser urzeitlicher Schmelzwasser-Seen hat weiches Gestein unter darüberliegenden Felsschichten ausgewaschen und so in Hunderten von Jahren diese bis zu 200 Meter tief ins Erdinnere hineinreichenden Höhlen geschaffen. Mit dem Abschmelzen der Eiszeit-Gletscher ging auch das Wasser, die Höhlenzugänge lagen frei. Und wurden natürlich entdeckt: Die Ureinwohner Patagoniens haben hier bereits vor 11.000 Jahren Schutz vor Wind und Wetter gefunden, auch von den großen Säugetieren einer heute untergangenen Zeit findet man Spuren. Der Name „Milodón" weist übrigens auf ein ausgestorbenes, pferdegroßes Riesenfaultier hin, von dem man in der größten Höhle Knochen entdeckt hat.

Die Zeitreise ins Erdinnere ist magisch. Und dann sind wir wieder in der Gegenwart unterwegs. Rollen voran, machen Meter. Nehmen Fahrt auf, Tempo, Tempo. Auf der RN9 nach Süden, während links und rechts die Tundra Patagoniens vorüberzieht, als Meditation in Monochrom. Betonplatten-Laufband mit gelbem Spur-Lidschatten, scharf auf den Horizont schießend. Wir sind eine Kugel, die mit 80 km/h den Lauf verlässt, geradewegs auf Puerto Natales zu. Sprit und Wasser fassen, dann in einer Lücke im Osten der Stadt durch die Hügelkette hindurch, die uns bis hierher begleitet hat. Hinter der kleinen Laguna Arauco schleicht sich die argentinische Grenze an, verschwindet dann aber doch in östlicher Richtung, wie mit dem Lineal gezogen. Wir huschen über den Rio Rubens, durchqueren dann Los Angeles ... Moment mal! Los Angeles? – Umdrehen, nachschauen. Und ja, richtig, die knapp zehn Häuser in einem Straßendreieck mitten in der Pampa heißen tatsächlich so. Auch wenn die urbanen Dimensionen etwas anders sind, kommen im Umland von „Los Angeles, Natales, Chile" wirklich nordamerikanische Gefühle auf: Die RN9 zieht mit dem selbstsicheren Vorwärtsdrang eines US-Highways dahin. Kerzengerade oder höchstens sanft geschwungen, auf üppig dimensioniertem Unterbau. Ein abgebrühter Profi des Meilenfressens. Kein Vergleich mit den dahingeprügelten Regenwald-Schotterpassagen der Carretera Austral weiter oben im Norden. Bis zum Rio Pendiente streben wir entlang der chilenisch-argentinischen

meltwater lakes has washed out soft rock under overlying layers of rock over hundreds of years to create these caves that reach up to 200 meters deep into the earth's interior. As the Ice Age glaciers melted, so the water also disappeared, exposing the cave entrances. Naturally, they didn't go unnoticed: the natives of Patagonia took shelter from wind and weather here 11,000 years ago, and there are also traces of the large mammals of a time long gone. Incidentally, the name "Milodón" refers to an extinct, horse-sized giant sloth, the bones of which were discovered in the largest cave.

The journey through time to the earth's interior is quite magical. And then we find ourselves back in the present. We push ahead, covering plenty of ground. We pick up speed, because it seems time is of the essence. Heading south on the RN9 with the Patagonian tundra sweeping left and right becomes a monochrome meditation. Our eyes are trained sharply on the horizon as we grind our way forward on a treadmill of concrete slabs. We veer off course like a bullet at 50 miles an hour, headed straight for Puerto Natales. We refuel and pick up some water, then burrow our way through a gap to the east of the city through the chain of hills that has accompanied us this far. Just beyond tiny Laguna Arauco, the border with Argentina comes into sight, but then disappears in an easterly direction, as if drawn with a ruler. We scurry across the Rio Rubens, then pass through Los Angeles... Wait a minute! Los Angeles? – We turn around for a second look. And yes, that's right, the almost ten houses in a triangle of streets in the middle of nowhere genuinely share a name with the City of the Angels, although the urban dimensions are slightly different. Nonetheless, there's a certain North American feel to the countryside around "Los Angeles, Natales, Chile": the RN9 moves along with the confident propulsion of a US highway. The road runs straight as an arrow or follows a gentle curve on a lavishly dimensioned substrate. We cover many miles in comfort: there is no comparison with the punishing rain forest gravel tracks of the Carretera Austral further north. We head east along the Chilean-Argentinian border to the Rio Pendiente, then the RN9 changes course, resolutely heading

PASO GARIBALDI

PASO GARIBALDI

PASO GARIBALDI

Grenze nach Osten, dann wechselt die RN9 ihren Kurs: entschlossen nach Süden. Bis Punta Arenas an der Magellanstraße sind es jetzt nur noch rund 150 Kilometer, die Straße zieht sich beinahe endlos durch sanft gewelltes Land. Aber dann wird es spannend: Die Laguna Cabeza de Mar ist ein erster Gruß des Atlantiks, der hier, mitten in der Pampa, natürlich kaum zu erkennen ist.

Erst ein Blick auf die Landkarte zeigt die Zusammenhänge: Im Norden der großen Wasserfläche schließt ein Kanal nach Osten an, der in die kleinere Laguna Verdana führt, und die ist über einen rund drei Kilometer langen Durchstich mit der Magellanstraße verbunden. Eben jener rund 600 Kilometer langen Durchfahrt zwischen Atlantik und Pazifik, die der portugiesische Seefahrer Ferdinand Magellan im Herbst des Jahres 1520 entdeckt hat. Und auf der man sich die Umrundung der Südspitze Südamerikas, die Mahlströme und Stürme am Kap Hoorn sowie 720 Kilometer Seereise ersparen kann.

Einige Kilometer weiter südlich treffen wir auf eine Entdeckung der Neuzeit: Ein großes Windrad dreht sich über der flachen Tundra-Landschaft, darunter ducken sich Industrieanlagen. Der nie stillstehende Wind des Südens erzeugt hier viele Megawattstunden Strom, seine Energie verwandelt Wasser und der Atmosphäre entnommenes CO_2 in Wasserstoff, der wiederum in Benzin, Diesel oder Kerosin umgewandelt werden kann. Sozusagen grün erzeugter Kraftstoff für Flugzeuge, Schiffe und Autos, die für einen anstehenden Umbau der globalen Mobilität nicht aufgegeben und wieder ressourcenfressend durch neue, alternativ angetriebene Flug- oder Fahrzeuge ersetzt werden müssen, sondern nachhaltig und CO_2-neutral bis ans Ende ihres Lebenszyklus weiter betrieben werden können. Die Rechnung bezahlt dabei der Wind Patagoniens: Ohne seine nahezu kostenlose Unermüdlichkeit würde in der energieintensiven Umwandlung von Wasser und CO2 in synthetischen Sprit die entscheidende Komponente fehlen, er lässt die eigentlich nicht wirtschaftliche Rechnung aufgehen. Noch ist die Anlage in der Prototypenphase, wird aber bald E-Fuel für ausgesuchte Anwendungen industriell erzeugen. Als wir auf der Fähre zwischen Punta Arenas und Porvenir über die Magellan-

Eben jener rund 600 Kilometer langen Durchfahrt zwischen Atlantik und Pazifik, die der portugiesische Seefahrer Ferdinand Magellan im Herbst des Jahres 1520 entdeckt hat. Und auf der man sich die Umrundung der Südspitze Südamerikas, die Mahlströme und Stürme am Kap Hoorn sowie 720 Kilometer Seereise ersparen kann.

This is the approximately 600-kilometer passage between the Atlantic and Pacific that the Portuguese seafarer Ferdinand Magellan discovered in the autumn of 1520 and that can save you from having to circumnavigate the southern tip of South America, the maelstroms and storms at Cape Horn and a 720-kilometer sea voyage.

south. It is now only about 150 kilometers to Punta Arenas on the Strait of Magellan, The road stretches almost endlessly through gently undulating terrain. But then things get exciting: the Laguna Cabeza de Mar is a first hallo from the Atlantic Ocean, but of course is barely recognizable as such here, in the middle of the pampas. A quick glance at the map shows the connections: a canal in the north of the large body of water links to the east, leading to the smaller Laguna Verdana, which is connected to the Strait of Magellan by a roughly three-kilometer-long passage. This is the approximately 600-kilometer passage between the Atlantic and Pacific that the Portuguese seafarer Ferdinand Magellan discovered in the autumn of 1520 and that can save you from having to circumnavigate the southern tip of South America, the maelstroms and storms at Cape Horn and a 720-kilometer sea voyage. A few kilometers further south we come upon a more modern discovery: a huge wind turbine turns above the flat tundra landscape with a number of industrial plants below it. The never-ending southerly wind generates many megawatt hours of electricity here, its energy converting water and CO2 taken from the atmosphere into hydrogen, which in turn can be converted into petrol, diesel or kerosene. This is green fuel for airplanes, ships and cars, which will not have to be abandoned as part of a forthcoming restructuring of global mobility to be replaced by

HOTEL & RESTAURANT

HOTEL LOS ÑIRES
AV. LOS NIRES 3040, V9410 USHUAIA, TIERRA DEL FUEGO

REINAMORA
UNNAMED ROAD, USHUAIA, TIERRA DEL FUEGO
WWW.LOSCAUQUENES.COM

Entlang der Bahia Inútil, einer weit ins Land gezogenen Bucht der Magellanstraße fahren wir nach Osten, erreichen kurz vor San Sebastian die Grenze nach Argentinien. Die trennt hier, wieder wie mit dem Lineal von Nord nach Süd gezogen, Feuerland in zwei Teile.

We drive east along the Bahia Inútil, a bay of the Strait of Magellan that extends far into the country, reaching the border with Argentina shortly before San Sebastian. Here, again as if drawn with a ruler from north to south, it divides Tierra del Fuego into two parts.

straße nach Feuerland fahren, ist uns im Schweröl-Duft des Schiffsdiesels schnell klar, dass eine automobile Perspektive auf alternative Antriebe vielleicht zu eng gefasst ist. Elektroautos könnten in gut vernetzten Ländern mit solide gemachter Infrastruktur ganz sicher eine Hauptlast individueller Mobilität tragen. Bei Schiffen oder Flugzeugen sieht die Sache etwas anders aus: Ladekabel reichen nicht auf den Ozean hinaus oder bis in die Tropopause. Bis Container-Schiffe also das Segeln neu erlernt haben oder Flugzeuge mit Wasserstoff fliegen, könnten E-Fuels eine Überbrückungstechnik sein und das windzerzauste Patagonien hilft beim Nachdenken.

Die Fähre bleibt im Hafen von Porvenir zurück, wir machen uns auf die letzten Kilometer unserer Reise. Feuerland. Beinahe geschafft. Entlang der Bahia Inútil, einer weit ins Land gezogenen Bucht der Magellanstraße fahren wir nach Osten, erreichen kurz vor San Sebastian die Grenze nach Argentinien. Die trennt hier, wieder wie mit dem Lineal von Nord nach Süd gezogen, Feuerland in zwei Teile. Ein letztes Mal reihen wir uns in die Grenzkontrolle zwischen den Staaten, die sich Patagonien teilen, und müssen an die anderen Querungen denken. Oben in den Anden. Im Regenwald. In der Pampa. Wenige Minuten später sehen wir den Atlantik, die weite Sichel der Bucht von San Sebastian. Rund 120 Kilometer weit folgen wir seiner Küste, dann geht es zurück zu den gebirgigen Fjorden, Seen und Inseln des Pazifiks: 60 Kilometer nach Süden, an die Ostspitze des Lago Fagnano, schließlich ein letztes Mal Kurven und Berge. Der Garibaldi-Pass bringt uns hinüber nach Ushuaia. Die südlichste Stadt Südamerikas.

new, alternatively powered aircraft or vehicles that gobble up resources. Instead, existing means of transport can continue to operate sustainably and CO2-neutrally until the end of their service life. The winds of Patagonia foot the bill: without their untiring, almost free contribution, we would lack the key component in the energy-intensive conversion of water and CO2 into synthetic fuel. It is the wind that allows the actually uneconomical model to work. The system is still in the early stages, but will soon be producing e-fuel for selected applications on an industrial scale.

When we take the ferry between Punta Arenas and Porvenir across the Strait of Magellan to Tierra del Fuego, the smell of heavy oil from the ship's engines quickly makes it clear to us that alternative drives are about more than just cars. Electric cars could certainly take the brunt of individual mobility in well-connected countries with solid infrastructure. Things are a bit different for ships or planes: charging cables in the ocean or in the sky are an impossibility. So, until container ships return to sail power or planes learn to fly on hydrogen, e-fuels could represent an interim solution, and wind-swept Patagonia offers plenty of food for thought.

We leave the ferry behind in the port of Porvenir and start the last part of our journey. Tierra del Fuego. We're almost there. We drive east along the Bahia Inútil, a bay of the Strait of Magellan that extends far into the country, reaching the border with Argentina shortly before San Sebastian. Here, again as if drawn with a ruler from north to south, it divides Tierra del Fuego into two parts. One last time we line up at the border control between the states that share Patagonia and have time to think about the other crossings. Up in the Andes. In the rain forest. In the pampas. A few minutes later we see the Atlantic and the wide crescent of the Bay of San Sebastian. We follow the coast for about 120 kilometers, then the road switches to the mountainous fjords, lakes and islands of the Pacific: 60 kilometers south, to the eastern tip of Lago Fagnano. One last chance to enjoy the curves and mountains. The Garibaldi Pass takes us over to Ushuaia, the southernmost city in South America.

Parque Nacional
Tierra del Fuego
BAHIA LAPATAIA
República Argentina
Aquí finaliza la Ruta Nac. N°3
Buenos Aires 3.079 Km.
Alaska 17.848 Km.

TORRES DEL PAINE USHUAIA

Die wilde und unvergleichliche Schönheit des Nationalparks Torres del Paine macht ihn zu einer der bekanntesten und meistbesuchten Gegenden Patagoniens. Wer den Park also nicht mit vielen anderen Besuchern teilen möchte, sollte trotz des dann eher sicheren Wetters mit Temperaturen bis 20 Grad Celsius und tendenziell weniger Niederschlag nicht im Sommer anreisen. Vorsicht bei der Planung: Wegen der Lage Patagoniens auf der Südhalbkugel liegen die Sommermonate im Dezember und Februar ... Für einen Besuch im Winter – also Juni bis August – sollte man sich auf kaltes und verregnetes Wetter einstellen, darüber hinaus sind die Tage ausgesprochen kurz. Der Frühling hat seinen Reiz, unser Geheimtipp wäre aber ein Besuch im Herbst, von März bis Mai. Jetzt verfärbt sich die Vegetation reizvoll, das Wetter kann sonnige Momente haben und Unterkünfte findet man auch noch etwas spontaner, ohne lange Vorbuchzeit. Auf unserem weiteren Weg nach Süden zeigt sich Patagonien aber ebenfalls von einer spannenden Seite. Selbst ohne die spektakulären Naturattraktionen der Parks in den Anden strahlt das weite Land der Pampa und Tundra eine eigentümliche und anziehende Ruhe und Tiefe aus, es ist dünn besiedelt und oft menschenleer. Ein kräftiger und stetiger Wind bläst uns ans Ende der Etappe: mit der Fähre über die Magellanstraße nach Feuerland. Hier, im Süden des Südens, endet unsere Reise in der südlichsten Stadt des Kontinents: Ushuaia.

The wild and incomparable beauty of Torres del Paine National Park makes it one of the most famous and most visited areas of Patagonia. Consequently, if you don't want to share the park with lots of other visitors, you shouldn't travel there in summer, despite the more predictable weather, with temperatures up to 20 degrees Celsius and less rainfall. Be careful when laying your plans: because of Patagonia's location in the southern hemisphere, the summer months are from December to February... For a visit in winter – i.e. June to August – you should be prepared for cold and rainy weather, as well as extremely short days. Spring has its charms, but our insider tip would be to visit in the fall, from March to May. That's when the vegetation changes color in an attractive way, the weather can have sunny moments and accommodation can be found a little more easily, without having to book long in advance. As we continue south, Patagonia also shows an exciting side. Even without the spectacular natural attractions of the parks in the Andes, the vast area of pampas and tundra exudes a peculiar and alluring calm and depth. It is sparsely populated and often deserted. A strong and steady wind blows us to the end of this stage: we travel by ferry across the Strait of Magellan to Tierra del Fuego. Here, in the very southernmost point, our journey ends in the most southerly city on the continent, Ushuaia.

1.022 KM • 2-3 TAGE // 635 MILES • 2-3 DAYS

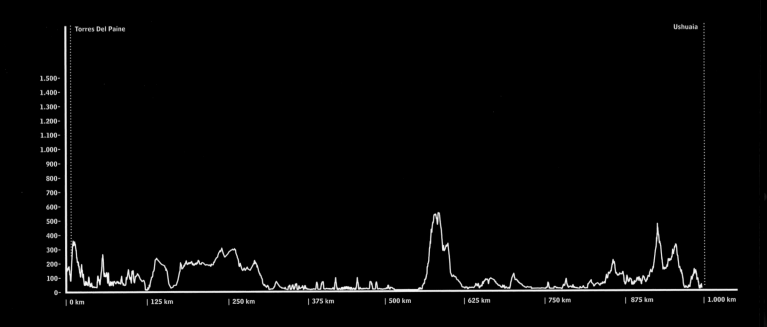

ASK THE LOCALS

Carlos, aka „The Commander", kennt die schönsten Straßen seiner Heimat mit Vornamen. Wie Ferdinand Magellan navigierte er uns sicher durch die einsamsten Gegenden Patagoniens, aka „The Nothingness", und erklärte uns dabei sehr charmant, dass man den Nordstern im Süden nicht sehen kann. Als Rallye-erprobte Tourmanagerin unserer Boygroup hat Colomba nahezu unbemerkt all das organisiert was einen perfekten Roadtrip ausmacht. Von der passenden Unterkunft über perfekte Food-Locations bis hin zu Grenzübergängen, die sich wie ein Spaziergang anfühlten. Big Smile!

—

Carlos, also known as "The Commander", knows the most beautiful roads of his home country like the back of his hand. Taking his lead from Ferdinand Magellan, he navigated us safely through some of Patagonia's loneliest places, also referred to as "The Nothingness", explaining to us with the utmost patience and charm that you can't see the North Star when you're down south. As our boy band's tour manager with rally experience, Colomba organized everything to make our road trip run like clockwork, from the right accommodation to the perfect food stops and border crossings that felt like a walk in the park. Big smile!

Drei Worte: Was macht Patagonien aus? *Colomba:* Größe, Frieden, Erhabenheit. *Carlos:* Veränderung, Landschaften, Kontraste.

Warum sollte jeder mindestens einmal in Patagonien gewesen sein? *Colomba:* Weil man dort die Großartigkeit der Natur in ihrer vollen Pracht erleben kann. Man fühlt sich einsam und klein inmitten der unermesslichen Weite. Es ist ein Ort, an dem sich wirklich alles real anfühlt: Wind, Regen, Kälte, Sonnenschein, Dunkelheit ... *Carlos:* Es ist einer der schönsten Orte der Welt, mit vielen unberührten Flecken und vielen landschaftlichen Veränderungen auf wenigen Kilometern. Ein abgelegener Ort, an dem man die Einsamkeit auf eine sichere Art und Weise erleben kann.

Wenn du keine Zeit hast, die gesamten 5.000 Kilometer von Nord- nach Südpatagonien zu fahren, was sind deine Lieblingsorte, die man gesehen haben muss? *Colomba:* Auf jeden Fall die „Carretera Austral" und ihre Umgebung: Yelcho, Puerto Marín Balmaceda, Puyuhuapi, Puerto Guadal, Caleta Tortel, um nur einige zu nennen. *Carlos:* Die gesamte „Carretera Austral" (Ruta 7), Parque Patagonia, Perito-Moreno-Gletscher und Torres del Paine.

Zwei Menschen pro Quadratkilometer: Was ist das Besondere an den Patagoniern? *Colomba:* Ihre aufrichtige und einfache Freundlichkeit und ihr Verständnis für Zeit. „El que se apura en la Patagonia pierde su tiempo", sagt man, was auf Deutsch so viel heißt wie „wer sich in Patagonien beeilt, verschwendet seine Zeit". *Carlos:* Ihre Freundlichkeit und ihr einfacher Lebensstil. Sie wissen, dass sie in einer rauen Gegend leben, deshalb sind sie immer hilfsbereit. Und sie sind immer aufgelegt für ein gutes Gespräch.

Patagonien ist eine Mischung aus ...? - Nenne drei andere Länder. *Colomba:* Die Alpen, Costa Rica und Australien. *Carlos:* Australien, die Alpenländer, Neuseeland.

Reisen in Patagonien: Welche Jahreszeit ist die beste? *Colomba:* November bis Dezember: Das Wetter ist schon sehr gut und es ist noch nicht so überlaufen. *Carlos:* Von November bis April. Die besten Monate sind November, Dezember und März, dann ist das Wetter am besten und weniger Menschen sind unterwegs.

Reisen in Patagonien: Welche drei Dinge sollte man unbedingt dabei haben? *Colomba:* Outdoor-Ausrüstung, Snacks und gute Musik. *Carlos:* Regenjacke, ein Multitool mit Messer und Zeit.

Was war das Schlimmste, das dir unterwegs passiert ist? *Colomba:* Schwierige Frage, wir hatten eigentlich keine

Three words: what defines Patagonia? *Colomba:* Greatness, peace, sublimeness. *Carlos:* Change, landscapes, contrast.

Why should everyone have been to Patagonia at least once? *Colomba:* Because you can experience the greatness of nature at its maximum expression. You feel lonely and small among the vast immensity. It is a place where everything feels really real: wind, rain, cold, sunshine, darkness... *Carlos:* Is one of the most beautiful places on earth, a lot of pristine places and a lot of changes in landscapes in a few kilometers. Is a remote place where you can experience loneliness in a safe way.

If you don't have time to drive the full 3,500 kilometers from north to south Patagonia, what are your favorite must-see places for visitors? *Colomba:* "Carretera Austral" and its surroundings, definitely: Yelcho, Puerto Marín Balmaceda, Puyuhuapi, Puerto Guadal, Caleta Tortel, just to mention some. *Carlos:* The complete Carretera Austral (Ruta 7), Parque Patagonia, Perito Moreno Glacier and Torres del Paine.

Two people per square kilometer: what is special about the Patagonians? *Colomba:* Their genuine and simple kindness and their understanding of time. "El que se apura en la Patagonia pierde su tiempo" is the premise, which in English would be something like "he who hurries in Patagonia, wastes his time". *Carlos:* Their kindness and simple lifestyle. They know they live in a rough area so they are always willing to help. And they are always happy to have a good conversation.

Patagonia is a mixture of...? – Name three other countries. *Colomba:* The Alps, Costa Rica and Australia. *Carlos:* Australia, the Alpine Countries, New Zealand.

Traveling in Patagonia: What time of year is the best? *Colomba:* November to December: the weather is already very kind and it is not that crowded yet. *Carlos:* From November to April. The best months are November, December and March, with the best weather and fewer people.

Traveling in Patagonia: What three things should you definitely have with you? *Colomba:* Outdoor gear, snacks and good music. *Carlos:* Rain jacket, a multitool knife, time.

What's the worst thing that has ever happened to you on the road? *Colomba:* Hard question, we had no problems at all. The hardest was the wind sometimes that would make things fly away, and doors slam. (But this was never really bad, it was great to feel it, actually.)

Probleme. Das Schlimmste war der Wind, der manchmal Dinge wegfliegen ließ und Türen zuschlug. (Aber das war nie richtig schlimm, es war sogar schön, ihn zu spüren.) *Carlos:* Bis jetzt hatte ich Glück, nur Reifenpannen und kleinere Probleme mit dem Auto oder dem Motorrad, da gibt es nicht allzu viel zu sagen …

Was ist das Beste, das dir auf deinem Weg passiert ist? *Colomba:* Wieder eine schwierige Frage. Die ganze Reise war eine Art spiritueller Einkehr. Vielleicht war das Beste, Kaffee und Snacks an Flüssen, Seen, Tälern und Wasserfällen zu trinken und die Brise zu spüren. *Carlos:* Neue Leute kennenzulernen und Freundschaften zu schließen. An Orte zu gehen, die einen tief in die Seele eintauchen lassen.

Mit welchem Reisebegleiter würdest du gern auf deine persönliche Patagonienreise gehen? *Colomba:* Natürlich mit meinem Freund! *Carlos:* Meine allerbeste Reise durch Patagonien war allein auf meinem Motorrad, aber wenn ich wählen müsste, würde ich meine Familie mitnehmen. Patagonien ist eine perfekte Familienreise.

Welche drei patagonischen Lieblingsspeisen sollten Besucher unbedingt probieren? *Colomba:* Königskrabbe, gebratenes Lamm und argentinisches Barbecue. *Carlos:* Königskrabbe, patagonisches Lamm Asado, lokale Biere.

Mit welchen Erwartungen sollte man auf keinen Fall nach Patagonien kommen? *Colomba:* Erwarte niemals, dass das Wetter stabil ist. Erwarte auch nicht, dass du viele neue Freunde findest und Partys feiern wirst. *Carlos:* Man sollte nicht mit einem festen und strengen Zeitplan kommen, alles kann sich in einer Minute ändern. Das Wetter ist unberechenbar, du willst an einen neuen Ort, von dem du gerade gehört hast. Es gibt viele Dinge, die sich ändern können, also sei flexibel.

Welches Land/welche Region auf der Welt würdest du am liebsten besuchen? Welches Abenteuer möchtest du erleben? *Colomba:* Ich würde gerne die gesamte Region Südostasien besuchen. Mein Abenteuer wäre wahrscheinlich, zu essen und mich von all diesen exotischen, wunderbaren Aromen verzaubern zu lassen! *Carlos:* Asien ist ein Mysterium für mich, das Essen und die Kultur sind etwas, das ich unbedingt ausprobieren möchte. Vielleicht ist der Himalaya die richtige Wahl für meine abenteuerlichere Seite, ich würde gerne die Basislager der großen Achttausender sehen.

Wenn du Patagonien für immer verlassen müsstest – wohin würdest du gehen? *Colomba:* Irgendwo nach Italien! Ich liebe die Intensität und Wärme Italiens. *Carlos:* In den Norden Spaniens, vielleicht nach Galizien.

Carlos: I've been lucky until now, just punctures and minor car or bike issues, not too much to say…

What's the best thing that's happened to you along the way? *Colomba:* Hard question, again. The whole trip was kind of a spiritual retreat. Maybe the best was having coffee and snacks by rivers, lakes, valleys, waterfalls and feeling the breeze. *Carlos:* Knowing new people and making friends. Going to places that let you dive deep into your soul.

With which travel companion would you like to go on your personal Patagonia trip? *Colomba:* My boyfriend, definitely! *Carlos:* My very best trip through Patagonia was alone on my motorcycle, but if I have to choose, my family is my choice. Patagonia is a perfect family trip.

What three favorite Patagonian foods should visitors try? *Colomba:* King crab, roasted lamb and Argentinian grill. *Carlos:* King crab, Patagonian lamb asado, local beers.

What kind of expectations should you absolutely not come to Patagonia with? *Colomba:* Never expect the weather to be stable. Don't expect to find a lot of new friends and to go partying either. *Carlos:* You should not come with a fixed and strict schedule, everything can change in a minute. The weather is unpredictable, you want to go to a new place you just heard about. There are a lot of things that can change, so be flexible.

Which country/region in the world would you most like to visit? What adventure to experience? *Colomba:* I would love visiting the whole South-East Asia region. My adventure would probably be eating and being captivated by all those exotic wonderful flavors! *Carlos:* Asia is a mystery for me, the food and culture is a thing I want to try. Maybe the Himalayas are the choice for my more adventurous side, I would love to see the base camps of the big eight-thousanders.

If you had to leave Patagonia forever – where would you go? *Colomba:* Somewhere in Italy! I love Italian intensity and warmness. *Carlos:* North of Spain, to Galicia maybe.

BAC KST AGE

Wir sind am Ende. Präziser: am Ende der Welt. Endlich angekommen. Das heißt, nicht ganz: Etwas über 5.700 Kilometer liegen an unserem Startpunkt im chilenischen Puerto Montt vor uns, bis wir unten im Süden, von Feuerland aus, nur noch den Blick auf eisgrauen Pazifik haben – nächster Stopp: Antarktis. Dazwischen liegt Patagonien. Und die Fahrt durch dieses wilde, atemberaubend schöne Land, zum südlichen Ende des amerikanischen Kontinents, ist so etwas wie die Reise in eines der letzten Paralleluniversen unseres Planeten. Ein immer unwirklicheres Vorantasten in stillstehende Zeit. Ein Traum aus unwirklicher Schönheit. Ein dauerndes Ankommen im Unterwegssein. Definitives Ende und stetiger Anfang in einem. Ungefähr so würden wir die Reise durch Patagonien umschreiben.

Wir, das ist eine kleine Gruppe von Reisegenossen, die sich aus den unterschiedlichsten Gründen einem Vorhaben angeschlossen haben, das zu Beginn nicht mehr als eine Vision ist. Ein Traum. Ein Ausstieg. Oder wie auch

We've come to the end, or, to be more precise, the end of the earth. Finally. But not quite: a little over 5,700 kilometers lie ahead of us at our starting point in Puerto Montt, Chile, until all that's left is a view of the ice-gray Pacific Ocean from Tierra del Fuego to the south. Next stop: Antarctica. Sandwiched in between is Patagonia. Our drive through this wild, breathtakingly beautiful country, to the southern end of the American continent, is something like a journey into one of the last parallel universes on our planet, an increasingly unreal probing of a place where time stands still. A dream of intangible beauty. A state of permanent arrival despite being constantly on the move. A definitive end and a steadfast beginning all in one. That's roughly how we would describe our journey through Patagonia.

We are a small bunch of traveling companions who, for a variety of reasons, have joined a project that was just a vision to begin with. A dream, an opportunity to drop off the radar, or however you wish to classify a plan to

immer man das Vorhaben nennen mag, in der Wildnis Patagoniens ans Ende der Welt zu fahren. Das ist nicht unbedingt eine All-inclusive-Kreuzfahrt mit festem Tagesprogramm und Abendunterhaltung. Eher das Gegenteil. Und diese Gruppe wird die Reise prägen, ihre Geschwindigkeit und ihren Verlauf, ihren Rhythmus und ihre Farben. Nicht umsonst nennen wir uns schon bald „Die Band". Denn genau das sind wir: vollkommen unterschiedliche Charaktere, die etwas zur Fahrt beisteuern – mindestens sich selbst. Und am Ende wird etwas entstanden sein, das es nur so gibt, weil diese ganz bestimmten Menschen aneinander auskristallisiert sind.

Die Mitglieder der „Band" nehmen ihren Platz ein, finden sich, rütteln sich auf den Schotterpisten Patagoniens fest. Es gibt die Philosophen und Navigatoren, die Bremser und Heizer, die Zweifler und Optimisten. Einige Gefährten gehören schon lange Zeit zum Team, zu CURVES on tour, Freunde der CURVES-Community klinken sich als Überraschungsgäste live on stage ein. Zwei neue Mitglieder der CURVES-Band haben den Gig in Südamerika besonders bereichert: Colomba und Carlos. Wenn Colomba lacht, verliert selbst der härteste Grenzbeamte seine strenge Miene und es kann passieren, dass man von ihm danach zum Fußballschauen in die gute Stube eingeladen wird. Dabei ist Colomba eigentlich eine Rallye-erprobte, talentierte Schauspielerin, die sich auf unserer Reise das Ukulele Spielen beigebracht hat. Dabei organisiert sie, fast unbemerkt, die perfekte Unterkunft, findet die nächste Tankstelle und würde niemals zulassen, dass jemand „hangry" wird. We love you, „Mama"! Carlos kennt Patagonien in und auswendig, als passionierter Adventure-Biker und Hiker demonstrierte er den ganz besonderen Riecher für Straßen, die es wert sind, erkundet zu werden. Wenn wir uns als Roadtripper etwas wünschen dürften wäre es wohl das Carlos-Plugin fürs Navigationssystem. „El Commandante" hat uns sicher und mit unendlicher Geduld an all diese wunderbaren Orte geführt und wir durften von ihm viel über das Land, die Natur und die Menschen lernen. Dass Carlos einen Pilotenschein hat, mehrfach die Schallmauer durchbrochen hat und quasi Stammgast in der Antarktis ist, haben wir auf der Reise so ganz nebenbei erfahren. „Totally" Carlos eben ...

Natürlich ist aber jede und jeder auf dieser Reise essenziell ganz besonders. Jeder Blickwinkel bereichert die Fahrt. Wir haben auf dem langen Weg ans Ende der Welt deshalb eine Gemeinschaft erlebt, die kostbar, sinnvoll und unentbehrlich war. Während ringsum die Welt Patagoniens zum dramatischen Hauptdarsteller wurde, der mit jedem Kilometer immer mehr alles zur Ruhe brachte und relativierte, uns Menschen auf sich selbst zurückwarf, das Innerste hervorholte. Die verschwenderisch weite Natur Patagoniens hat etwas klarzustellen: Menschen sind auf diesem Planeten Gäste. Mehr nicht. Leben ist ein Privileg, keine Selbstverständlichkeit. Gut auch, dass wir uns für die lange Fahrt

drive to the end of the world in the wilderness of Patagonia. This isn't necessarily going to be an all-inclusive cruise with a set daily program and evening entertainment. Rather the opposite in fact. This group is going to shape the journey, its speed and direction, its rhythm and its colors. It's not for nothing that we call ourselves "The Band". Because that's exactly what we are: a group of completely different characters all of whom bring something of themselves to the journey. And in the end something will have emerged that only exists because these very specific people have gelled.

The members of "The Band" find their place, getting to know each other and naturally molding themselves into a cohesive bunch on the dirt roads of Patagonia. We have philosophers and navigators, cautious souls and thrill-seekers, doubters and optimists. Some of our companions have been part of the team for a long time, regulars when CURVES goes on tour, while others are friends of the CURVES community who join us live on stage as surprise guests. In particular, two new members of the CURVES band have enriched the gig in South America: Colomba and Carlos. When Colomba laughs, even the toughest border official will drop his stern expression and may even invite you to watch football in his living room afterwards. Colomba is actually an experienced rally driver and talented actress who taught herself to play the ukulele on our trip. Almost unnoticed, she organized the perfect accommodation, found the nearest gas station and would never allow anyone to get "hangry". We love you, "Mama"! As a passionate adventure biker and hiker, Carlos knows Patagonia like the back of his hand and demonstrated a very special instinct for which roads were worth exploring. If we road trippers could wish for something, it would be to have a Carlos plugin for the navigation system. "El Commandante" guided us safely and with infinite patience to all of these wonderful places and gave use the opportunity to learn a lot from him about the country, its nature and people. On the trip, we found out that Carlos has a pilot's license, has broken the sound barrier several times and is a regular visitor to Antarctica. "Totally Carlos" you might say...

Of course, each and every one of the people on this trip is essentially very special. Every different perspective enriches our journey. Thus it was that we experienced a community that was precious, meaningful and invaluable on the long trek to the end of the world. Meanwhile, all around us the world of Patagonia took on the role of dramatic protagonist, calming and relativizing everything more and more with every passing kilometer, throwing us humans back on ourselves and bringing our innermost being to the fore. The extravagantly vast natural riches of Patagonia have a clear message for us: we humans are guests on this planet, nothing more. Life is a privilege,

ideale Reisegenossen der automobilen Kategorie ausgesucht haben: Auf den brachialen Schotterpisten und Gebirgspässen Patagoniens, diesen vielen Kilometern als Traumwandlern, waren die Porsche Cayenne der ersten Modellgeneration einfach genial. Durchsetzungsfähig und energiegeladen, komfortabel und groß, ebenso mit flinker Beinarbeit ausgestattet wie mit beeindruckendem Fassungsvermögen. Mächtige Kofferräume mit Rallye-Talent. Reise-Elefanten, die bei Bedarf gewaltig voranstürmen können und dann wieder die Stetigkeit selbst sind.

Und noch etwas gehört zu dieser Reise: Bereits die Anreise zum Startpunkt der Fahrt in Chile ist aus unserer europäischen Perspektive keine banale Flugverbindungsangelegenheit, sondern eine Pilgerfahrt mit tiefer Wirkung. Es dauert schließlich selbst in Jet-Geschwindigkeit viele Stunden, bis man aus der Mitte Europas die großen Städte Südamerikas erreicht hat, und auch hier ist man immer noch unfassbar weit von Patagonien entfernt. Am Flughafen von Buenos Aires oder Santiago de Chile angekommen, hat der Reisende jenen Zustand zwischen Lethargie und distanzierter Selbstbeobachtung erreicht, den Fernreisen oder Flüge zum Mars eben bei der Spezies Homo sapiens auslösen: Du ahnst, dass du nicht hierher gehörst, aber dass umdrehen und nach Hause zurückschleichen nun auch keine Option mehr sind. Dann stehst du neben dir an den Anzeigetafeln der Fluglinien, schlafwandelst durch die Terminals. Dabei hüllen sich deine Synapsen in eine pelzige Jetlag-Aura und du stellst fest, dass es bis zum Beginn Patagoniens immer noch mehrere Stunden Warten und erneutes Fliegen sind. Oder auf alte Bahnverbindungs-Währung umgerechnet: tagelange Reise. Diese Erkenntnis des Verdammt-weit-weg-Seins sickert langsam ein, kommt als eiskalter Schock oder als zähfließender Fatalismus, und wenn du in diesem Moment der Erkenntnis irreversibler Verlorenheit so etwas wie Freude empfindest, weißt du: Ich liebe es, unterwegs zu sein. Weil Menschen unserer Sorte eben nicht gern stehenbleiben, deshalb. Weil es manchmal überhaupt nicht weit weg genug sein kann. Am Ende gehörte dann sogar der Heimweg zu den schwierigsten Etappen unserer Reise nach Patagonien, weil dieses magische und wunderschöne Land Menschenseelen einsaugt und nur unvollständig wieder hergibt. Am Ende der Fahrt sind wir immer noch voller Andacht und Sprachlosigkeit. Keine andere Reise hat uns bisher so von innen nach außen gedreht, etwas ist für immer in Patagonien geblieben. Bittersüß fernwehschmerzend.

Wie das geht? Sein Herz an eine Landschaft verlieren und diese Erfahrung als Geschenk betrachten? – So ganz haben wir das immer noch nicht verstanden. Nur, dass ein Teil von uns immer noch auf der Anden-Passhöhe auf dem Weg nach Bariloche steht, an den Fjorden des Rio Cochrane, am Fuß der Torres del Paine oder am Beagle-Kanal. Am Ende der Welt. Oder: an ihrem Anfang.

not something to be taken for granted. It's also a good thing that we chose the right vehicles as traveling companions for the long journey: the first generation Porsche Cayenne models were simply brilliant on the brutal gravel roads and mountain passes of Patagonia, carrying us as if in a dream. They displayed an assertive energy, offering plenty of comfort and space and combining nimble agility with an impressive luggage capacity. These mighty pack-elephants are ideal for rally conditions, pushing ahead at speed if necessary and then becoming the epitome of dependability and continuity once again.

There is something else that is an intrinsic part of this journey: from our European perspective, getting to the starting point of our journey in Chile is not simply a matter of making flight connections, but in fact a profound pilgrimage. After all, even at jet speed, it takes several hours to reach the major cities of South America from the middle of Europe, and even here we still have a long distance to travel before we reach Patagonia. Arriving at the airport in Buenos Aires or Santiago de Chile, travelers find they have reached that state somewhere between lethargy and distant introspection that long-haul journeys trigger in mankind as a species. It is almost like being on a flight to Mars: you suspect that you don't really belong here, but turning around and sneaking back home is no longer an option. You then find yourself standing in a stupor, gazing at the airline display boards, sleepwalking your way through the terminals. Your synapses are enveloped by jetlag's fuzzy embrace as you realize that there are still several hours to wait before flying on again and before Patagonia begins. In the old days when the railway was king, this journey would have taken several days. The realization that you are far, far away from home slowly begins to seep in, coming as a blood-curdling shock or a nagging fatalism. If you feel anything even akin to happiness at the moment you realize your irreversible abandonment, then you know that you're a dyed-in-the-wool wanderer. People like us simply hate to stand still. Sometimes you just can't get far enough away from it all. In the end, the way home was actually one of the most difficult stages of our trip to Patagonia, because this magical and beautiful country draws in the human soul and only gives part of it back again. At the end of our trip we are still full of silent, reverent awe. No other trip has turned us inside out like this and part of us stayed behind in Patagonia forever. The bittersweet pain of wanderlust.

How does it happen? How do you lose your heart to a landscape and consider the experience as a gift? – We still haven't quite understood it. All we know is that part of us is still standing at the top of the Andes on the road to Bariloche, by the fjords of the Rio Cochrane, at the foot of the Torres del Paine or staring out over the Beagle Channel. At the end of the earth. Or is it the beginning?

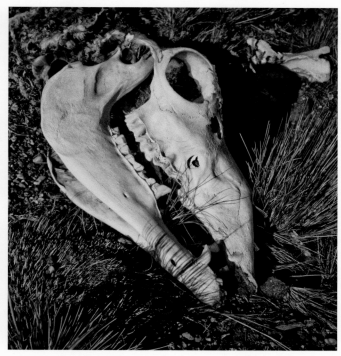
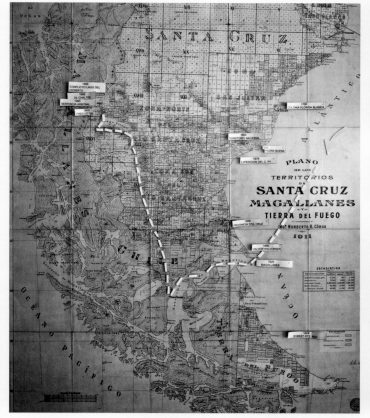

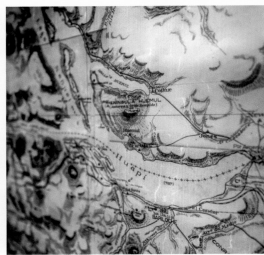

LEICA SL-SYSTEM
EINE WEGWEISENDE ENTSCHEIDUNG

Als Ergebnis von über 100 Jahren deutscher Ingenieurskunst bietet das SL-System optische Spitzenleistungen und ermöglicht es Fotografen und Filmemachern, außergewöhnliche visuelle Arbeiten zu erschaffen. Lassen Sie sich von diesem Meisterwerk der Handwerkskunst inspirieren und erzählen Sie Ihre Geschichte wie kein anderer es kann.

Entdecken Sie unbegrenzte Möglichkeiten unter sl-system.leica-camera.com

 MOUNT |  CAPTURE ONE PRO | Lr Adobe Photoshop Lightroom | CINE LENSES

DANK AN / THANKS TO

Porsche Latin America, Jan Kuppen, Barbara Scarabello, Ingomar Jaeger, Esteban Rico • Porsche Chile: Vicente Díaz, Nicole Avila, Marcos Pimstein, Iván Lichnovsky, Nicolás Borquez, Cristóbal Lüttecke • Horta Producciones: Colomba Horta, Carlos Gaete, Cesar Norambuena • Maximilian Ramisch, Bastian Schramm • Ben Winter, Nadja Kneissler, Axel Gerber, Hanno Vienken, Michael Dorn, Michaela Bogner

SPECIAL FX / SPECIAL FX

David Steca, Matthias Wagner & Frank Thiele
Horta Producciones: Colomba Horta & Carlos Gaete for their help and friendship

CURVES TRAVEL AGENT:

AOT Travel • info@aottravel.de • Tel. +49 89 12 24 800

IMPRESSUM / IMPRINT

HERAUSGEBER/
PUBLISHER: CURVES MAGAZIN
THIERSCHSTRASSE 25
D-80538 MÜNCHEN

VERANTWORTLICH FÜR
DEN HERAUSGEBER/
RESPONSIBLE FOR
PUBLICATION:
STEFAN BOGNER

KONZEPT/CONCEPT:
STEFAN BOGNER
THIERSCHSTRASSE 25
D-80538 MÜNCHEN
SB@CURVES-MAGAZIN.COM

DELIUS KLASING
CORPORATE PUBLISHING
SIEKERWALL 21
D-33602 BIELEFELD

REDAKTION/
EDITORIAL CONTENT:
STEFAN BOGNER
BEN WINTER

ART DIRECTION, LAYOUT,
FOTOS/ART DIRECTION,
LAYOUT, PHOTOS:
STEFAN BOGNER

MAKING OF FOTOS:
MICHAEL DAIMINGER

TEXT/TEXT: BEN WINTER
TEXT INTRO/TEXT INTRO:
BEN WINTER

MOTIVAUSARBEITUNG,
LITHOGRAPHIE, SATZ/
POST-PRODUCTION,

LITHOGRAPHY, SETTING:
MICHAEL DORN

KARTENMATERIAL/MAP
MATERIAL: MAIRDUMONT,
OSTFILDERN

ÜBERSETZUNG/TRANSLATION:
JAMES O'NEILL

PRODUKTIONSLEITUNG/
PRODUCTION MANAGEMENT:
AXEL GERBER

DRUCK/PRINT:
KUNST- UND WERBEDRUCK,
BAD OEYNHAUSEN

1. AUFLAGE/1ST EDITION:
ISBN: 978-3-667-12497-5

AUSGEZEICHNET MIT / AWARDED WITH

DDC GOLD – DEUTSCHER DESIGNER CLUB E.V. FÜR GUTE GESTALTUNG 2011 // IF COMMUNICATION DESIGN AWARD 2012
BEST OF CORPORATE PUBLISHING 2012 // ADC BRONZE 2011 // RED DOT BEST OF THE BEST & D&AD // NOMINIERT
FÜR DEN DEUTSCHEN DESIGNPREIS 2015 // WINNER AUTOMOTIVE BRAND CONTEST 2014 // GOOD DESIGN AWARD 2014

CURVES AUSGABEN / OTHER ISSUES OF CURVES

PYRENÄEN
PYRENEES
Im Handel erhältlich/Available in stores

ÖSTERREICH
AUSTRIA
Im Handel erhältlich/Available in stores

SCHWEIZ
SWITZERLAND
Im Handel erhältlich/Available in stores

SCHOTTLAND
SCOTLAND
Im Handel erhältlich/Available in stores

FRANKREICH
FRANCE
Im Handel erhältlich/Available in stores

USA · KALIFORNIEN
USA · CALIFORNIA
Im Handel erhältlich/Available in stores

SIZILIEN
SICILY
Im Handel erhältlich/Available in stores

NORDITALIEN
NORTHERN ITALY
Im Handel erhältlich/Available in stores

OSTDEUTSCHLAND
EASTERN GERMANY
Im Handel erhältlich/Available in stores

NORDITALIEN
NORTHERN ITALY
Im Handel erhältlich/Available in stores

DEUTSCHLAND/DÄNE.
GERMANY/DENMARK
Im Handel erhältlich/Available in stores

SPANIEN · MALLORCA
SPAIN · MALLORCA
Im Handel erhältlich/Available in stores

USA · COLORADO/UTAH
USA · COLORADO/UTAH
Im Handel erhältlich/Available in stores

THAILAND
THAILAND
Im Handel erhältlich/Available in stores

SÜDDEUTSCHLAND
SOUTHERN GERMANY
Im Handel erhältlich/Available in stores

PORTUGAL
PORTUGAL
Im Handel erhältlich/Available in stores

NORWEGEN
NORWAY
Im Handel erhältlich/Available in stores

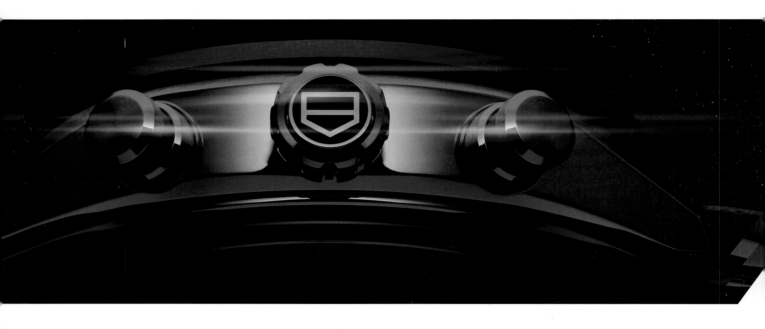

Adrenaline
comes as standard.

TAG HEUER CARRERA

Porsche Chronograph